US Army M113s on the move in Samarra, Iraq. (SSgt Shane A. Cuomo, US Air Force)

ACAVs adopt a defensive herringbone formation behind an M48, Vietnam. (Donn A. Starry)

INTRODUCTION

The M113 Armoured Personal Carrier (APC) is part legend part icon, instantly recognizable. The M113 is equally at home supporting advances across rice paddies, or tearing across expanses of desert. Indeed, the M113 is as much a recognizable part of the US military machine as the 'Huey' and the M16.

The M113 earned its stripes in the humid jungles and highlands of South Vietnam, becoming the most widely utilized armoured vehicle of the campaign. It fulfilled a range of roles, from APC to command post and everything in between; on occasion damaged M113 hulls were mounted onto the cargo beds of M54 trucks creating a hybrid gun-truck. Used to protect the numerous fuel and ammunition convoys that traversed South Vietnam, these hybrids ensured the convoys fed the many camps and fire bases. Indeed, such was its ability to travel anywhere in the field that the Viet Cong nicknamed the M113 the 'Green Dragon'.

The key to the M113's success is the simplicity of its design and innate versatility. Built around a ground-breaking armoured aluminium alloy hull, which is able to protect occupants against small-arms fire and artillery shrapnel, the M113 weighs a mere 12 tonnes. This light weight also allows it to be easily transported by air as well as being amphibious. Over the years a wide range of enhanced armour packages have been used to complement the aluminium armour, from the humble sandbag to complex appliqué armour.

This wonderful shot of a German Panzermörser M113A1G showing off its unique NATO tricolour camouflage scheme.

An M113 and Humvee on IFOR duties in Bosnia encounter some heavy going. (US Army)

Above: US infantrymen on exercise dismount from an M113 in 1985. (US Army)

One edge that the M113 has maintained is that it is exceptionally easy to modify, enabling it to carry a wide range of support and indirect-fire weapons. From mortars to ballistic missiles, the M113 family of vehicles (FoV) has spawned a progeny of useful and innovative assets. Indeed, such was its popularity that the US military bought their final M113s in 2007 when the M113 family made up 40 per cent of a US heavy brigade's tracked combat vehicles.

As testimony to the excellence of its design, born from experience and keeping all changes simple, some 80,000 M113s, of all types, have been produced by manufacturers worldwide. This vast family of vehicles can be found in use in over 50 countries, making the M113 one of the most widely used AFVs ever produced. Such is its popularity that the M113, with updates and enhancements, will remain in service with some armies until the 2050s.

For the modeller the M113 represents an absolute goldmine of inspiration and opportunity as well as the possibility of producing some wonderful camouflage finishes. From UN peacekeeping missions to Cold War dioramas based in Central Europe to iconic action-packed Vietnam vignettes, the M113 really is a great foundation for creative modelling. If ever there was an APC that came complete with its own fast-paced, 1960s-inspired soundtrack, then the M113 would be that vehicle.

Below: An early Second World War dismounted infantryman kneeling in front of an M3 halftrack, holds and sights an M1 Garand rifle. Fort Knox, Kentucky, June 1942. (Library of Congress)

Design & Development

The design and development of the M113 can be traced back to the battlefields of the Second World War which had delivered a great many lessons in modern warfare to all belligerents, including the need for the total mechanization of ground troops. It had also proved that such platforms should be flexible and easily convertible to a variety of roles, including mortar and anti-tank gun carrier. However, two key factors were identified: the need for total mobility and total protection.

The continual track rather than the halftrack of wartime APCs had been proved to be the optimal method for moving cross-country. This new generation of APCs should also be amphibious, much like the US Landing Vehicle Tracked (LVT) Buffalo, but without the high profile and weight disadvantages. The use of improved armour and designs were also incorporated into the APCs, the most noticeable being the return to the enclosed box on tracks approach, which echoed the British Mk IX troop carrier of the First World War.

This enclosed design approach not only protected troops against airbursts, but in the technological age, kept troops relatively safe from nuclear, biological and chemical attacks with a range of protective systems. The M75 was the first of this new generation of tracked APCs to enter service with the US Army in 1952. It could trace its lineage back to the ill-fated post-war M44, which could carry up to 24 troops, but whose 23-tonne size was prohibitive. This led to a return to the drawing board and in September 1945 a new design brief was released.

In September 1946 the development of the new APC, known at this stage as the T18 Armoured Utility Vehicle, was approved with a contract to produce four prototypes, awarded to International Harvester (IHC) by the Springfield Armory. The T18 was to be constructed from a welded steel hull, with thickness from 25mm to 38mm; the front hull had a line-of-sight thickness of between 40mm and 50mm and it could carry 14 troops, including crew. It was also fitted with two remote-controlled .50-cal guns which were controlled by either the vehicle commander or two designated gunners.

As the project progressed several changes were introduced: T18E1 was unarmed, and the commander was treated to a raised

The British First World War Mk IX Armoured Personnel Carrier Tank, Tank Museum, Bovington.

cupola. While the prototypes were intended to be unarmed, T18E2 included a T122 twin .50-cal gun mount, similar to that found on the M24 Light Tank, which was capable of carrying a .30-cal gun. The M13 cupola was also evaluated: mounting a .50-cal gun, it was similar to the M1 cupola that was later fitted onto the M48 Patton, and included the awkward clamshell-like rear access hatch.

All four prototypes were initially powered by a Continental AO-895-2, horizontally opposed 6-cylinder air-cooled petrol/gasoline engine. This was replaced by

The Continental AO-895-4 6-cylinder horizontally opposed, air-cooled petrol engine that powered the M75 is seen here on its sliding mount that assisted with maintenance. (Alf van Beem)

the AO-895-4 engine which produced an impressive 295hp, giving the T18 a top speed of 43mph (69km/h). The T18 carried 568 litres of fuel, giving it a range of around 115 miles (185km). The T18 was equipped with a cross-drive transmission and the driver was able to steer its tracks through

The US Army's first practical APC, the M75, introduced in 1952, would see action in Korea, before being withdrawn from US service in 1960. It remained in service with the Belgian Army into the 1980s. (Ryan Crierie)

The troop exit for the M75 wasn't perhaps the most practical, but it seemed to work. (Alf van Beem)

The M59 would bring the experiences gained from the M75 as well as a new tradition of continuous development to post-war APC design. While not perfect, it was a step in the right direction. (Mark Pellegrini)

two steering levers. The suspension was torsion bar type which works by twisting with the road wheels' vertical movement, providing the vehicle with an improved spring action. Each side of the T18 was fitted with five road wheels and three return rollers. Interestingly, the T18 shared a great many chassis and component elements of the M41 Walker Bulldog, including the torsion bar suspension.

In 1952, after field trials, the T18E1 was ordered into production to become the M75. An initial order for 1,000 units was placed with IHC with a further 730 produced by the Food Machinery and Chemical Corporation (FMC). For FMC, who had produced tracked vehicles during the Second World War, including the LVT, this would be great opportunity to hone their skills in producing the next generation of APCs.

Before production could start there were changes required to help reduce unit cost and complexity. Two shock absorbers were fitted per side instead of the original four, along with an auxiliary generator/heater. The two 75-gallon rubber fuel tanks were replaced by a single, more robust and sensible 150-gallon metal one. The M75 was initially on par with its predecessors in terms of power-to-weight ratios: the 1941 M3, weighing 9.07 tonnes, produced 16.2hp/tonne while the M75 APC, which was almost 10 tonnes heavier at 19.5 tonnes, produced 16.3hp/tonne. By the time the M113 arrived in 1960 with a 12.3-tonne weight, it was producing 22.4hp/tonne.

The M75 driver was seated on the port side of the hull, with the power pack to his right, an arrangement which would find its way into use with the M113. He was provided with four M17 periscopes and, in later models, the M19 infrared night vision periscope was also available. To the rear of the driver sat the commander, his centrally mounted cupola provided with six vision blocks. The commander's cupola could be fitted with an M2 Browning, for which 1,800 rounds were carried. Up to 12 troops were seated behind the commander, with entry and exit facilitated by two doors placed in the rear of the body. Two roof hatches were fitted and could be set at differing heights, as well as fully open, to allow troops to observe and fire safely.

None of this came cheap, and with a unit cost of $72,000, the M75 production run was cut short at 1,729 units. Other factors included its high profile and lack of an amphibious capability, although it could ford to a depth of 120cm or 200cm with a wading kit. Yet the M75 and its battlefield experience in Korea had proved that the concept of the new generation of APCs worked.

Interestingly, no sooner had the M75 completed its field trials than the US Army approached FMC in 1951 to start working on a series of replacements. The

Fitted with an M13 cupola and an extended trim vane, this M59 clearly shows how the designers were slowly getting there in terms of shape and style. (Joe Mabel)

best-performing design, the T59, made by FMC, was chosen from a series of prototypes, and named the M59, and ordered into production in 1953.

The M59 built and improved on many of the features of the M75; in appearance it was a scaled-down version, retaining the boxlike structure of the M75. The hull was constructed from welded steel with thicknesses ranging from 9mm on the roof to 25mm on the belly. It was powered by two GMC Model 302 six-cylinder inline petrol engines generating a combined power output of 292hp.

Both engines were connected to a General Motors Hydramatic 301MG transmission (4F1R) with torsion bar suspension attached to five road wheels with shock absorbers fitted to the first and last road wheels. Like the M75, the steering was via controlled differential via steering levers. The twin engines were mounted in the M59's sides, accessible from inside or via roof panels. Practically, it must have been awkward to maintain in the field and the synchronization arrangement proved to be unreliable. The M59 carried 511 litres of petrol/gasoline, giving it a range of approximately 120 miles (150km). The vehicle was designed to be amphibious, and was equipped with rubber-sealed hatches and doors as well as a front-mounted trim vane. In the water, it had a maximum speed of 4.3mph (6.9km/h).

The M59 had an open interior with the driver again positioned on the left, with the vehicle commander seated to his right. The driving position retained all the visual driving aids that had been furnished for use on the M75 and the commander was again given the M13 cupola, with a .50-cal M2. The rear compartment held 10 troops with overhead hatches provided; seats were side-mounted, and could be folded to allow the carriage of a Jeep. Entry was either a single centrally mounted door set into the large single-piece ramp or the downward hinging ramp itself.

The M59 was lacking in a lot of areas in which the M75 excelled and paradoxically was virtually the same weight as the M75 at 19 tonnes. Its top speed of 32mph was 11mph slower than its predecessor; its light armour and separate engines were never going to be easy to live with. That said, it was cheaper, costing $32,000 per unit, and 6,300 were produced, including the M84 Mortar Carrier variant. The M59 served from 1954 into the 1980s, seeing active service in Vietnam alongside the M113.

In 1954, with experience from the Korean War and field use of the M75 and M59, the US military was keen to see the APC concept refined. The world had changed greatly since the first plans for the next generation of APCs were drawn up, so the development of the replacement would be exhaustive. Another possible influencing aspect in the design of the new APC can be found in the 1954 essay 'Cavalry, and I Don't Mean Horses' written by General James Gavin.

Gavin, the former commander of the 82nd Airborne Division, was an exponent of a lighter, more agile form of airborne-based cavalry warfare. In the essay he wrote:

> Cavalry is supposed to be the arm of mobility. It exists and serves a useful purpose because of its mobility differential—the contrast between its mobility and that of other land forces. Without the differential, it is not cavalry. Cavalry is the arm of shock and firepower: it is the screen of time and information. It denies the enemy that talisman of success—surprise—while it provides our own forces with the means to achieve that very thing, surprise, and with it destruction of the enemy.

The Korean conflict had shown that there was more than a grain of truth to Gavin's ground-breaking doctrine. When faced with

Above left: Lieutenant-General James M. Gavin's 1954 essay predicted a lighter more agile way of warfare using APCs a decade before it became doctrine in Vietnam. (US Army)

Right: The US 8th Cavalry Regiment prepare to attach an M113 to a CH-47 helicopter at Fort Stewart. (SSgt Elvis N. Umanzor, US Army)

Below: The new APCs were similar in appearance to the M59, but that's where the similarity ended.

Centre: The full M8A3 CBRN system carried by the M113.

Bottom: These early prototypes show growing refinement of the concept. Note the lack of idler wheel on these vehicles.

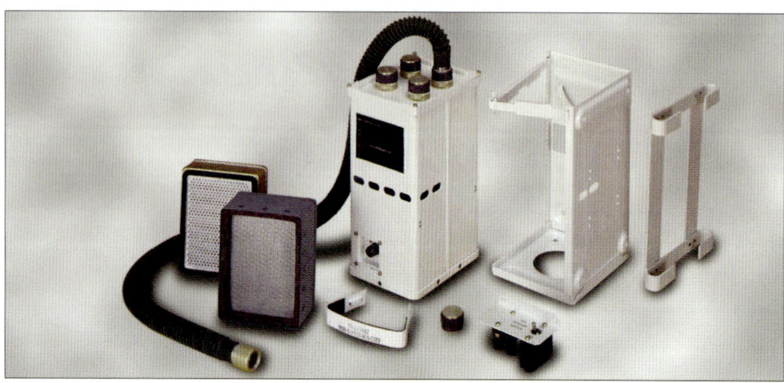

the difficult Korean terrain, heavy armour formations were of little tactical use, and were often relegated to defensive roles.

Gavin argued these lighter and more easily deployed formations could be carried into combat by aircraft and backed up his argument with his own experiences as well as historical precedents where light cavalry had won through. He envisaged a force that, once deployed, would rush to complete its objectives overwhelming the enemy though speed and agility, supported by air assets, and then retrieved by heavy aircraft and helicopter.

This new doctrine wasn't initially popular among the general staff of one of the most powerful armies in the world; after all, it was proposing lighter strike forces as Gavin felt that the massed armies which had swept their way through Europe had had their day. These revolutionary ideas certainly gained traction beyond the military and the M113 clearly echoed Gavin's theories. Indeed, such was Gavin's influence on the design that there was a campaign to have the M113 called *Gavin*. This followed the American military tradition of naming armoured vehicles after generals. Sadly, it came to nothing.

As a result, though perhaps not as a consequence of Gavin's new ethos, one key design change was as an air-portable platform, known as Airborne Armoured Multi-Purpose Vehicle Family (AAM-PVF). This family of vehicles would be made in wheeled and tracked versions, and based on two differing weight platforms. The first was to be a 'light' platform weight, approximately 3.6 tonnes, while the other would be 'heavy', weighing approximately 7.6 tonnes.

These ideas were in development and in June 1955 a presentation was made to the Continental Army Command (CONARC), with the proposed 10-man tracked APC remodelled so that it would take 12 personnel instead (two crew and 10 troops). The following January CONARC approved the development of a tracked family of vehicles which would carry 13 personnel and named the T113. Alongside this project would be a smaller version, the T114, which would carry four personnel, plus a few wheeled variants. This later became the M114 Command and Reconnaissance Carrier, seeing service from 1962 to 1973 before being replaced in the reconnaissance role by the M551 Sheridan.

As well as being air-portable, the need for an all-terrain and amphibious capability remained, and the tactical doctrine that had developed meant that the new APC would act as a battlefield taxi to charge into the combat area, deploying troops, before rapidly withdrawing. For operating in an area that may well have been subjected to nuclear, biological and chemical weapons, the T113s and subsequently the M113s provided the crew with an NBC protection system. As an overpressure-type system was not compatible with the nature of operating an APC and the size of the T114/M113 would inhibit the fitting of a large filtration unit, a smaller unit (33 x 15 x 19cm) was installed. This consisted of an M8A3 gas-particulate unit with an M2A2 air purifier, with flexible hose assemblies which carried purified air to the four M14A1 tank gas-mask respirators for the driver, vehicle commander and two others. However, the system could not filter carbon monoxide nor could it provide oxygen to protect against asphyxiation.

FMC was awarded the contract to construct 16 examples of the new vehicles for evaluation in May 1956, with half the vehicles to be made from aluminium and powered by an air-cooled engine. The others were to be constructed from steel and powered by a liquid-cooled engine. The reasons for using differing power packs was not noted, but one can presume that CONARC felt that a lighter air-cooled engine would be far more suitable powering the aluminium-bodied vehicle than a liquid-cooled engine. While easier to maintain, air-cooled engines are prone to overheating, and suffer from poor efficiency as they run a slightly richer fuel/air mix, which would preclude it from powering the steel-hulled variants. All 16 vehicles were to be built in a range of variants: 10 APCs, two mortar carriers, three missile carriers and a single experimental chassis. In October 1956 the mock-up of the T113 was completed and after inspection the production of the APC and mortar test vehicles was approved.

The layout of the T113 placed the driver once again in the front left with the commander behind, where he had access to a centrally located hatch. The commander was equipped with a single ring-mounted .30-cal gun, the only form of firepower. Next to the driver was the engine, along with the transmission and final drives, which

allowed the area behind the commander to be utilized purely for troop carriage. The fuel tank, initially located in the front right corner of the body, along with the exhaust and air intakes, was later moved to the rear left-hand side of the vehicle in production models.

Like the M59 the T113/T117 would run on five road wheels, utilizing the same torsion bar suspension and rubber-padded T130E1 track. The rear idler and front drive sprockets were new and designed specifically to enable improved handling as opposed to the M75's and M59's reused M41 components. The main form of suspension was that of torsion bar and as long as the track was well maintained and kept taut, the T113 could still travel cross-country, even with a broken torsion bar. However, this system was supplemented by external shock absorbers mounted on the leading and rear road wheels, as well as the idler wheel. As a result of using torsion bar suspension, the road wheels were slightly staggered in their alignment, meaning that the left-hand side consisted of 63 links, while the right consisted of 64. This number of track links remained on the production M113s, excluding the six-wheeled A4 model which had six extra links either side.

Like the M59, the passengers were seated on inward-facing benches placed along the sides of the vehicle; above them was sited a single, large rectangular hatch which opened rearward. Like the M59, personnel could exit from the vehicle either via a powered ramp, or if under effective enemy fire via a rectangular door set into its left-hand side.

For the T113 the armour was 32mm on the roof, sides and upper and lower hull plates. For the vertical hull plate it was 44.5mm thick, a mere 9.5mm for the belly and 19mm for the lower hull sides. Overall, this gave the basic T113 hull a weight of 3.5 tonnes, just below the 'light' platform weight.

For its part the T117 employed rolled steel homogeneous armour of a modified hardness that, like the T113, was welded together. The armour for the main hull front and sides was 12.7mm, the vertical nose plate was 16mm, the belly plate 4.8mm and the lower hull sides 9.5mm. This gave the T117's hull a basic weight of 4.3 tonnes.

The next phase was to test the designs, with the armour test being done first; this started in 1957 and was completed in four phases. The first was to test the impact of 105mm HE shell fragments at varying distances. The second looked at the effect of impacts of 37mm and 57mm rounds. The third test involved small-arms fire, and the fourth and final test looked at the effects of bullet fragmentation around critical openings. The tests revealed a range of shortcomings for both designs: the T113's roof could be penetrated by 105mm

M113s of the 11th Armored Cavalry Regiment undertaking scout training at Fort George G. Meade, Maryland, in 1965. (US Army)

Above: An early shot of M113 driver training, Fort Jackson, SC, 20 June 1966. (US Army)

Below: Australian M113s moving forward in single file during Operation Smithfield, 19–22 August 1966, Long Tan, Vietnam. (Australian War Memorial)

fragments and when fired at close proximity (12.5m away) the same fragments could also penetrate the armour of the steel-bodied T117. The flank armour on both was found to be easily pierced at close proximity, and both prototypes suffered weld cracking when subjected to shock tests. However, both showed resilience to small-arms fire, including armour-piercing rounds.

Unsurprisingly, the T117 with its steel body fared far better than the light T113; however, as a result of the tests the T113 was to benefit from an increase in armour that allowed it to match the protection performance of the T117. Troop testing followed at the US Army's Aberdeen Proving Ground, Maryland: the primary test involved the ease in which troops could ingress and egress the prototypes. These tests were comparative against the still-in-service M59 with one test being a timed dismount. For the M59 it was 8.5 seconds against the T117's 9.5 seconds; the entry was also a second slower, though in part this could be put down to troop familiarization.

This activity aside, the main failings of the T113/117 were purely ergonomic: the driver had to perform a minor feat of gymnastics and contortion to get to his controls, and the rear seating could trap personal equipment. A key safety failing was that an open commander's hatch prevented the adjacent cargo hatch above the troop-carrying bay from opening. Given this hatch was a key emergency exit, it was back to the drawing board.

Left: The Armoured Cavalry Assault Vehicle (ACAV) reflected the changes the US military had to make to doctrine as a result of combat experience in Vietnam. (US Army)

Below: A young GI sits ready to roll in *Lee Anne*. Note the front shield of the commander's turret has been removed to prevent fouling the M40's barrel. (Bill Rambow)

The design brief was further altered by CONARC in 1957 by new budget limitations to key systems. The revisions required were reviews of the power pack while improving the armour, which was to remain aluminium, but using the new 5083 aluminium alloy. 5803 aluminium alloy was developed early in 1957 when FMC had begun working with Kaiser Aluminium and Chemical Company. It was a mix of magnesium with traces of manganese and chromium which could be easily welded and was exceptionally strong. It was capable of resisting small-arms fire as well as shell splinters, and produced a vehicle that provided the protection of the M75 with the low weight and mobility of the M59. This also ensured that the air-portable properties of the aluminium body were fully exploited.

As a result of the change of design brief, the development of the T117 was stopped and in October 1958 the new 5803-bodied prototypes became the airborne T113E1 'light' variant weighing 7.94 tonnes, and the heavier T113E2 weighing 10.9 tonnes. Both were powered by a Chrysler 75M petrol engine delivering 209hp. On both vehicles the engines were initially attached to a General Motors TX-200 manual gearbox, which was changed to an Allison TX-100-1 automatic transmission (3F1R).

Other key changes were a redesigned hull that was now distinctly M113 in shape. The vertical face plate was now gone and a retractable plywood trim vane for amphibious operations was now in place. Combined with tracks providing motive power, the T113E1 and E2 could be propelled though the water at 3.6mph. Finally, the original trailing idler wheel was now replaced with a raised idler wheel.

After much manoeuvring the troop capacity was increased to 11 while the armament remained a single .30-cal commander's gun. Testing continued at FMC's own facilities and the army's Aberdeen Proving Ground with the T113s being put through their paces to check cross-country performance. It was able to tackle gradients of 60 per cent, side slopes of 30 per cent, and had the ability to cross a 170cm trench and climb a 600mm step with ease.

By January 1959 testing was complete and it was the T113E2 which came out on top. However, CONARC requested that 181kg be shed from the T113E2's overall weight; these savings came from thinning various sections of the rear hull, floor and sponsons. Two further T113E2s incorporating the changes were produced for testing. These must have been successful as in April 1959 the T113E2 was adopted by the army, becoming the M113 Standard

'A'. It now replaced the M59 as the army's main APC with production starting in 1960.

By 1963 the M113 had been exposed to action for the first time with the Army of the Republic of Vietnam (ARVN). These M113s had been supplied as a batch of 32 in early 1962 to update two mechanized rifle companies. While welcome in support action against Communist forces, field use had highlighted a deadly design flaw. During the Battle of Ap Bac some 14 of the .50-cal gunners were killed as they exposed themselves to fire their guns.

This hastened the ARVN to think on their feet to improve battlefield survivability of their gunners and as a result shielding, sourced from the steel hulls of old ships, was added. Sadly, this was to prove of little use, so shielding was salvaged from scrapped armoured vehicles. The idea was sound but needed refinement, and so the evolution of the M113 began.

Using their field experiences the ARVN 80th Ordnance Unit developed a series of upgrades to improve protection and performance. The shield designs were refined and turned into a standard pattern that was the forerunner of the Armoured Cavalry Assault Vehicle (ACAV). These new shields were then fitted to all ARVN M113s.

As well as operating as a reconnaissance vehicle, the ARVN's M113 fleet started to change its role from mere APC to light tank. Here the emphasis was on firepower first, armed with heavy machine guns and on occasion the M40 106mm recoilless rifle. In this new role the infantry were viewed as support personnel who could dismount and take the fight to the enemy, before remounting and moving on to the next task. This new approach, although not quite what US advisors had taught the ARVN, helped to shape the doctrinal of how the M113 would be used, leading to the development of the ACAV, ironically much in line with Gavin's 1954 proposal.

With the arrival of US conventional forces in 1965, the new ACAV in its role as a light tank was further refined. Initially each M113 was fitted with three gun shields, designed and made in Okinawa. These shields consisted of a centrally mounted shield set which, once the commander's hatch was open, would form a type of open-topped turret. Behind this were flank-shielded M60 gun positions, accessed via the open rear cargo hatch and manned by the on-board troops. However, when the M40 106mm recoilless rifle was fitted on the right flank, the commander's front gun shield had to be omitted as it could foul the M40's barrel.

Soon the ACAV kits were standardized and from 1966 they were mass-produced in the US, with the design further refined. In some instances, the rear M60 mounts were omitted and the M113 converted to the M106 mortar-carrier role. Nearly all ACAV kits were field fitted apart from those M113s used by the 11th Armored Cavalry Regiment, who trained in the US with their ACAV kits. Interestingly, the ACAV kits would still be in use some 40 years later in Iraq.

Above: A commander from 2nd Battalion, 9th Cavalry Regiment peers over his ACAV shield during Operation Swarmer, Samarra, Iraq. (SSgt Alfred Johnson. (US Army)

Right: The M113 C&R Lynx, the first private venture by FMC to develop a derivative of the M113 was an export success. (Andrew Skudder)

Another vital in-theatre addition was improved mine protection for the vulnerable belly. Initially this consisted of sandbags placed over the floor, a practice which remained in use even after steel armour was bolted into place. One reason for the continuation of this practice was that the amour ran from the leading edge of the belly, finishing two-thirds of the way toward the rear.

Outside of the ACAV upgrade the first main development of the M113 by FMC was the Lynx reconnaissance vehicle in 1963. Known as the M113 Command and Reconnaissance Vehicle, or M113 C&R, the Lynx was specifically designed and built as a reconnaissance armoured fighting vehicle. It used the same 5083 aluminium armour as the M113 as well as elements of its construction. With the reduction of tread wheels from five to four, the Lynx was understandably shorter in length (4.6m) and lower in height (2.2m); it was also lighter, weighing in at 8,700kg.

One significant change was the relocation of the engine, which was offered in both petrol and diesel versions, and moved to the rear of the hull. While retaining all the amphibious abilities of the M113, crews would dispense with deploying the trim vane and bilge for slightly more than shallow wading, often storming a water obstacle at speed, which must have been an experience given its slightly faster speed of 44mph.

The M113 C&R was entered into a US Army competition to meet the requirements of a tracked reconnaissance vehicle against the General Motors M114. However, it lost to the M114, but was offered to foreign buyers. The Canadians named it the Lynx; it was also bought and operated by the Dutch Army.

The biggest mechanical change for the M113 came in 1964 with the introduction of a diesel-powered 6V-53 Detroit engine. Not only did this produce 210hp more power, but extended the range to almost 311 miles (500km). The new diesel-powered M113 would be known as the M113A1, with the 'A1' identifier being used on all diesel-powered variants of the M113 family.

The next side project of the M113 by FMC was in response to the Mechanized Infantry Combat Vehicle, 1965, or the MICV-65 project, designed to seek a replacement for the M113. This new project would see the US Army's drive towards a purpose-built Infantry Fighting Vehicle (IFV) as opposed to an upgraded APC like the ACAV. Among the contenders were FMC with their unique take on the idea, the XM734 or Mechanized Infantry Combat Vehicle (MICV). The XM734 was essentially an M113 with the side seating replaced by a centrally mounted bench. Troops sat outward and were able to observe the battle environment through four vision blocks under cover: underneath the blocks were ports out of which weapons could be fired.

While the XM734 lost out to a competitor's model, FMC was more than

FMC's entry into the competition for the new Mechanized Infantry Combat Vehicle or MICV-65 was little more than an upgraded M113. (US Army)

The Advanced Infantry Fighting Vehicle (AIFV), whilst funded by the US Army, was not adopted for use, but like the Lynx, it became an export success for FMC. (Rasbak)

Dutch AIFV and M113A2 in Bosnia as part of the Dutch Army's IFOR commitment. Note the rear fuel tanks. (Sgt Angel Clemons)

While heavily researched, the GRP hull concept remained just that and was shelved after inconclusive results. (Hunnicutt)

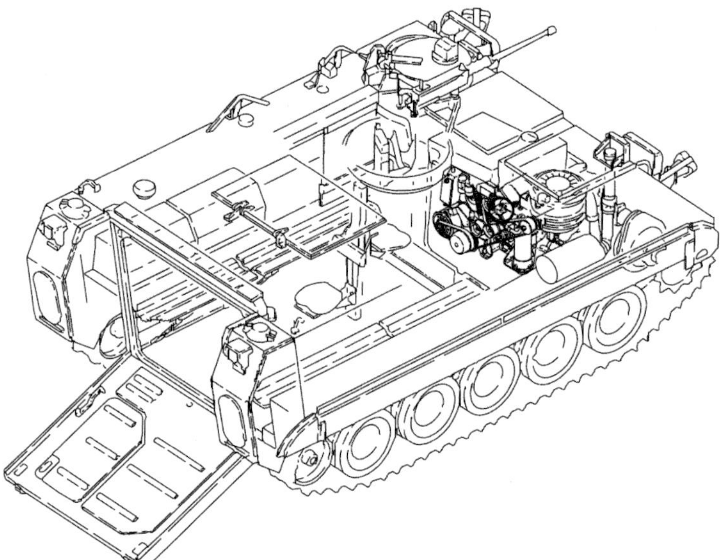

A cutaway of the new A3 RISE version. Note the spall liners have been pushed forward towards the driver's position.

happy with the concept and in 1967 the US Army funded FMC so the concept could be further developed, as the MICV-65 had been shelved. FMC's new model, the XM765, would be developed into the Advanced Infantry Fighting Vehicle (AIFV). The AIFV, with its fully enclosed one-man turret, wouldn't be ready for use until 1975, the same year that US involvement in Vietnam ended. While not used by the US military, the AIFV found favour with the other militaries, including the Turkish, Belgian and Dutch armies.

Around this time the post-Vietnam reports on the performance of military equipment had been fed back to designers, developers and manufacturers. As a result, FMC introduced the new A2 version in 1979. The A2 encompassed a huge range of vital modifications including an improved engine-cooling system achieved by repositioning the fan and radiator. Suspension was upgraded with stronger torsion bars and shock absorbers, which not only made for a smoother ride but increased the ground clearance from 409mm to 434mm.

Another key recognition feature was the introduction of armoured fuel tanks from the troop compartment to either side of the rear ramp, which freed up valuable

space for equipment stowage. A useful self-defence addition to the A2 was the inclusion of two M243 smoke grenade launching systems located midway on the front glacis plate. These changes came with a weight gain for the A2: 11,343kg against the A1's 10,920kg. This weight gain affected the hull's freeboard in the water so the amphibious requirement was dropped. Clearly this was not seen as a disadvantage as many A1s were upgraded to A2 standard.

One interesting development, and perhaps driven by British use of GRP armour in Northern Ireland, was the GRP Hull Feasibility Study undertaken by the USMC and FMC in 1983. The idea was to produce an M113 made from composite plastics. The first two hulls were produced by FMC with the Owens-Corning Fiberglas Corporation, who had a great deal of experience in the production of complex fibreglass-based composites. At the same time, Martin-Marietta, an aerospace company, conducted parallel research. The project became known as the Surface Mobility Program, or SURFMOB.

The test vehicles were to feature a GRP-constructed hull, as either a skeleton or sandwich material. In the case of the FMC/Owens-Corning project, a resin-bonded E-glass skeleton, covered with closed-cell polyurethane foam, and finished with aluminium oxide tiles was used. E-glass was chosen for its stability as well as capability of withstanding chemical agents (some chemical weapons are corrosive) while remaining dimensionally stable under variations in humidity and temperature.

Martin-Marietta chose to use an epoxy-sealed woven E-glass GRP body spliced onto the lower hull of the M113. The new body could then be finished with Alumina ceramic tiles, which had a range of properties that would make it attractive to the military user including heat resistance, cost and low weight.

The main purpose of the exercise was to save weight, but sadly, for all their efforts, both projects saved very little; in fact, the FMC/ Owens-Corning hull actually was 27kg heavier than the original aluminium body. Other issues included an increased repair time of battle damage; even minor repairs could take 24 hours, and considerable longitudinal twisting of the hull was also noted, though this lessened when the hull was fully equipped as a working M113. Benefits included ease of production, and better thermal properties. However, the range of engineering complexities, and associated costs that came with using a GRP-based hull were deemed too great. Overall, the project delivered some useful information, but never went beyond the research phase.

While the SURFMOB project was underway, it was clear that the M113 family was starting to show its age. As it had proved its usefulness time and again, the desire to extend its operational life was far

Left: Soldiers of the California Army National Guard (CAARNG) exit the back of their A3 to provide cover as other members of their unit move onto the house of suspected insurgents, Balad Air Base, Salah Ad Din Province, Iraq. (USAF TSgt Steve Faulisi)

Below: Soldiers from Team Bravo, TF 1-26 Infantry, 2nd Brigade Combat Team, 1st Infantry Division, use the A3's power to recover an overheated M113 in Hohenfels, Germany. (SPC Billy B. Brothers)

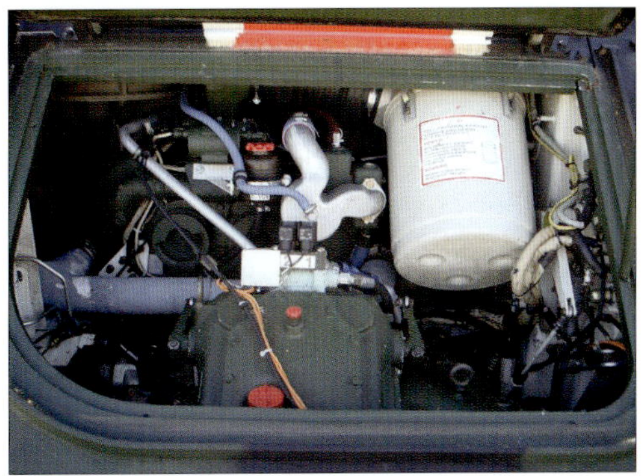

The M2-beating Detroit Diesel V6 certainly fills the engine bay originally designed for a flat 6.

greater than the need to withdraw it from service. In 1984 a life extension programme was launched, designed to add another 20 years' service life to the M113. Known as RISE (Reliability Improvements for Selected Equipment), the project undertook an impressive range of upgrades from motive power to crew projection.

The main change was the introduction of a new powertrain that had been developed and tested at both the Yuma and Aberdeen Proving Grounds: the 275hp turbocharged Detroit Diesel 6V53T. This came with a new 200-amp alternator, and was coupled to the new X200-4/4A hydrostatic steer transmission (4F2R). This arrangement removed the need for a transfer case and controlled differential. This change allowed the A3 to maintain sustained speeds of 41mph (66km/h) on level roads and a marked decrease in its 0 to 35mph time from 69 seconds to a staggering 27 seconds. To show how effective these changes were, a 'fun' drag race between the new 275hp M113A3 (22hp/tonne) and the 600hp M2A2 Bradley (22hp/tonne) was held at FMC's San Jose plant. The new A3 was the winner, by a country mile, so to speak.

As well as boosting acceleration, the RISE power pack also improved relative fuel economy, hill-climbing speed and braking capabilities. It also allowed the vehicle to maintain speed through corners by accelerating the outer track, which had been previously braked on the A2 version. Another benefit of the increase in engine power was that the A3 could carry and had provision for mounting external appliqué armour. While such a fit would increase the A3's overall weight to 14,061kg, it could still afford it as its mobility was comparable to the M2/M3 Bradley IFVs.

The RISE programme saw the driver treated to new power brakes and an automotive-style steering yoke and foot brake arrangement, which lessened fatigue and simplified the training process. Due to load-matching ability and increased steering capability, the cross-country performance of the A3 was also improved.

Internally the crew and passenger survivability were enhanced by the addition of a series of interleafed spall suppression liners. Made up of four large rail-mounted armour panels, that could be moved for access to non-critical kit and to

The six-wheeled A4 developed by United Defense was an overseas hit. Here an Australian A4 sits ready for inspection. Note the T150F tracks. (Nick Dowling)

This beautifully evocative still of an M113 Armoured Medical Evacuation Vehicle (AMEV) is also a great study shot, showing the exposed tracks and recently serviced road and idler wheels. The side skirting is often removed to prevent the clogging up of muck and debris. (SPC Timothy Jackson, US Army)

expand stowage, the liner acted as a form of spaced armour. While only effective against non-penetrating rounds, the liner reduced the size of the spall cone made by a ballistic impact, limiting the damage to personnel and vital vehicle systems. The rear-mounted fuel tanks were fitted with a unique valve system which continued to provide fuel should one tank be damaged.

From 1987 until the end of production in 1992, all M113s were built to A3 standard, and this new categorization was also extended to vehicles of the M113 family converted after 1989. Not only was this cost effective – a refurbishment cost $160,000 against the $300,000 purchase price of a new unit – it also meant existing vehicles could be brought up to spec.

Following the peace dividend that came with the ending of the Cold War, FMC merged its defence business with fellow defence manufacturer, Harsco Corporation's BMY Combat Systems Division in December 1992. BMY Combat Systems Division's expertise lay in the production of tracked vehicles, including the popular M109A2 Self-Propelled Howitzer. So, the merger made complete sense, especially given FMC's production of the Bradley IFV family of vehicles as well as the M113. In January 1994 the new company, United Defense,

emerged and among a host of transferred assets from FMC was the M113 production and its development lines.

The first project of United Defense was to develop the basic M113A3 design, initially called the M113A3+ or Mobile Tactical Vehicle Light (MTVL). The main visual difference between the MTVL and the M113A3 was the addition of an extra road wheel which resulted in the hull being lengthened by 860mm, but also added 4,000kg to the overall hull weight. The Detroit Diesel 6V53T power pack was changed to an extraordinarily powerful, electronically controlled Detroit Diesel 6V-53 TIA power pack. This new engine was a turbocharged, intercooled and after-cooled unit capable of developing a staggering 400hp. The hull, still built from 5083 aluminium armour, was developed to enable it to carry an optional appliqué armour package. This package provided protection against attack from 30mm armour-piercing projectiles over the M113's frontal arc. The armour set included upper and lower glacis and side plates made from titanium or steel tiles, while the belly was given spaced laminate steel. Other changes included the location of the fuel tanks, which could be carried externally, or under the floor in specially designed non-rupture fuel cells. Both external and internal fuel tanks could be mounted for a total fuel capacity of 757 litres.

The US military weren't interested in the new MTVL as they were focusing on the Bradley family of vehicles; however, the idea was adopted by Australia, Egypt and Turkey, becoming known as the M113A4. Each nation had local production facilities so retooling costs would be kept to a minimum. The Canadians ordered their A4s direct from United Defense, with 183 vehicles converted to the new standard. Indeed, Turkish arms company, FNSS Savunma Sistemleri A.Ş, continues to produce the M113A4 as well as it maintaining its own capability and sustainability programmes for

Mediterranean and South West Asian users.

In 2005, United Defense was acquired by BAe Systems, who continue to work with M113 users in over 40 countries, to roll out capability and sustainability programmes involving upgrade to powertrain and armour as well as protection improvements. Some countries such as Belgium, Italy and Taiwan have built the M113 under licence, and Australia, Israel and Singapore have been able to modify their fleets to fulfil local needs. With so many M113s still in service around the world, it's clear that the M113 will remain operational for at least another 30 years in some form or another.

Following is a selection of countries that have adapted and developed their own fleets of M113s into versions that may be of interest to the modeller. These variants are available as kits, aftermarket parts or can be readily converted from standard kits by the enthusiast.

Australia

The Australians adopted the M113 from 1966 during their involvement in the Vietnam War, and in time they would end up with a fleet of some 840 vehicles. Of these several key variants were developed as a result of their in-theatre combat experiences.

The M113A1 Light Reconnaissance Vehicle (LRV)/APC was a standard M113A1 fitted with a Cadillac Gage T50 turret similar to the type fitted to the Cadillac Gage Commando V100 series of armoured cars. This small turret was able to mount a range of machine guns, including, twin Brownings, a .30 cal and an M2 .50 cal. Used by cavalry and armoured regiments the LRV was manned by three crew: a

driver, commander and observer, as well as dismountable personnel. Given that the LRV had seating removed to carry extra stores, the interior space must have been tight.

The Fire Support Vehicle (FSV) or Carrier, Fire Support, Full Track M113A1 (FS) Saladin Turret, also known as 'The Beast', was another Vietnam-era variant. Retrofitted with the turret from the now-redundant Alvis Saladin armoured car fleet, the FSVs provided vital fire support for operations in the Australian Areas of Responsibility. The FSV was armed with an L5A1 76mm gun, a .30-cal coaxial machine gun and a .30-cal machine gun mounted on the roof of the vehicle's turret; it also retained the turret's useful smoke-grenade launchers. Very much an example of thinking 'on the hoof', the FSV was replaced by the M113A1 Medium Reconnaissance Vehicle (MRV) in the mid-1970s.

Like the FSV, the MRV or Carrier, Fire Support, Full Track M113A1 (FS) Scorpion Turret replaced the ageing

Above: With its sleek Scorpion turret and contemporary three-tone camouflage scheme, the MRV means business. The side sponsons and trim vane are foam-filled to aid buoyancy during water crossings.

Left: The FSV was a unique approach to providing troops with a defensive punch.

Saladin turret for the sleeker turret from the FV101 Scorpion light tank armed with the 76mm L23A1 gun. Fully amphibious, the MRV featured light sheet-metal, foam-filled trim vane and side pods that provided additional flotation and stability. Other changes included a modified driver's hatch that pivoted towards the centreline of the vehicle as opposed to swinging rearward, thus fouling the turret. Another vital modification was the inclusion of a 'boiling vessel', or BV. The BV is a small electric vessel used for boiling water and heating rations. The importance of a BV cannot be underestimated as a vehicle with a defective BV is declared unfit for purpose.

M113AS4 is the Australian version of the M113A4 vehicle fitted with a 'one-man turret', locally designed and produced by Tenix Defence, now BAe Systems. This low-profile, electrically driven turret features a 12.7mm heavy machine gun and sight. One key development by BAe Systems of the six-wheeled A4 has been the development of a series of armoured vehicles including the Armoured Logistics Vehicle (ALV) and Armoured Recovery Vehicle Light (ARVL) variants.

Canada

Canada first purchased the M113 in the mid-1960s and has since bought over 1,100 units. Over the years the M113 has been developed to produce a range of interesting variants. These include the unique MTV-E (Mobile Tactical Vehicle Engineer) with its front-mounted plough blade as well as hydraulics capable of powering a mounted auger and a range of hydraulic tools.

Another variant of interest to modellers is the ADATS Carrier (Air Defence Anti-Tank System). This unique multi-role defence system was developed collaboratively between Lockheed Martin and Oerlikon Contraves. The missile itself was laser-guided with a range of 6.2 miles (10km) and capable of speeds of Mach 3. The M113 was fitted with a suite of sighting aids including Forward Looking Infra-Red (FLIR) as well as a search radar with an effective range of over 15.5 miles (25km). The system was mounted on a 360° turret which carried eight tube-launched missiles, and associated sensors.

Israel

The Israel Defence Forces are one of the largest users of the M113 family, having had some 6,000 units of the type at their disposal over a 40-year period. Like other countries, the Israelis have developed a variety of versions to meet their own unique needs.

The Hafiz is an M113 equipped with a Spike NLOS ATGM launcher. The Spike, also known as 'Tamuz', is an electro-optic missile anti-tank and anti-personnel missile fitted with a tandem-charge HEAT warhead. As well as being operator-guided, the Tamuz is also capable of independently tracking both stationary and moving targets as a fire-and-forget system. The six-tube launcher, with 360° rotation, sits over the rear passenger compartment and is guided onto its target by the operator who is seated in the converted passenger compartment. Due to its capabilities the Hafiz is a devastatingly powerful and accurate piece of kit.

The Machbet is an Israeli Aircraft Industries development of the M163 VADS. As well as carrying the powerful 20mm M61 Vulcan rotary cannon, it is armed with a four-tube FIM-92 Stinger surface-to-air missile launcher. The Machbet is equipped with an upgraded tracking system with a capacity to establish a datalink to an external radar source. The rectangular launcher tube sits on the right-hand side of the VADS mount and is able to swing through 360°. The vehicle carries 1,800 rounds of 20mm ammunition for its M61 cannon and eight Stinger missiles.

Urban Fighter is an Israel Military Industries development of the M113 equipped with 'Iron Wall' armour which is capable of repelling Improvised Explosive Devices (IEDs) and explosively formed penetrator (EFP) attacks. As well as being up-armoured, the Urban Fighter has seen

The ADATS seen here at the Royal Nova Scotia International Tattoo with its optical tracking device in the foreground – an impressive piece of hardware. (JAH)

Orthodox Jewish soldiers pray atop their M113 Nagmash Toga. (David Horesh)

Designed to maximize the M113's amphibious qualities, the Arisgator is equally at home at seas as it is on land. (ARIS)

the M113's hull heavily modified with large windows set into the front and side of the hull to give clear views of the surrounding environment. In place of the commander position is a large enclosed viewing turret with excellent 360° vision.

Italy

As a licensed producer of the M113 family, the Italian firm OTO Melara, now part of part of the Finmeccanica conglomerate, has built 4,000 examples of the APC. As well as producing the basic M113 OTO, Melara also produced some 800 examples of the AIFV. These versions, known as the VCC- 1 and VCC-2, are fitted with revised rear and side-sloped armour, and include two viewing and two firing ports situated either side of the hull's troop compartment, Browning M2 shields and smoke-grenade launchers.

The SIDAM 25 is a self-propelled anti-aircraft weapon developed by mounting a large turret with four Oerlikon KBA cannon onto the remodelled hull of re-roled M113s. The Oerlikon's range is around 2,500m and is capable of firing 2,440 rounds per minute. The turret-mounted cannons have access to 150 rounds of high-explosive fragmentation ammunition each. A further internal magazine carries 40 armour-piercing discarding sabot (APDS) rounds for use against enemy vehicles. The turret rotates through 360° with the guns capable of being elevated to 87° or lowered 5° from the horizontal position. 276 have been built with a further 150 converted to carry the Oerlikon's 25mm ammunition.

One final interesting development is the Arisgator Light Amphibious Vehicle made by the Italian company Aris. The Arisgator takes the M113's amphibious qualities and develops these into a fully certified blue-water vehicle. Powered by two hydrostatically driven propellers, each mounted in their own stern sponsons and a remodelled bow, the Arisgator is testimony to Italian design flair. The Arisgator is in service with the Italian Navy's 'San Marco' Navy Brigade.

Taiwan

As well as operating some 650 imported M113s in a variety of roles, Taiwan (Republic of China) has also designed a range of M113-based vehicles with 1,000 produced by the Republic of China Armoured Vehicle Development Center between 1982 and 2009. These are similar in appearance to the AIFV and the base model is known as the CM21. Thus far there are six variants of the CM-21 including Mortar Carrier, CM-22/23 and TOW Launcher, CM-25.

A CM-21 APC taking visitors for a ride while simultaneously showing off its troop-carrying capacity. (Xuan Shisheng)

M113 in Detail

Sergeant Major of the Army William A. Connelly is introduced to the M113's engine by Sergeant Adderley of the 11th Armored Cavalry Regiment, V Corps.
(SPC Wilbert Wong Jr.)

NASA battalion chief David Seymour briefing crewmembers of Space Shuttle *Atlantis* before mission STS-135. It shows how cramped the interior really is even with the commander's seat post removed. Lots of detailing here for the keen-eyed modeller to soak up.
(NASA/Kim Shiflett)

Note the plywood trim vane of the ROCA A1. The light with the black lens is the infrared lamp and tracks are the early T130E1 types, identifiable by the 'T' form of the track pad. (Xuan Shisheng)

Aside from technological and mechanical developments, the basic M113 model has changed very little from its original design. While minor, there have been physical changes and these not only help the modeller to identify which mark of M113 they are building but also help produce an accurate model.

Approaching the M113 from the front, the modeller is met by the trim vane, where fitted, which comes in two separate styles: the simple flat plywood plate or the enlarged foam-filled style seen on the A2 and A3 versions. For those M113s that were later A1 or A2 and finished in camouflage patterns, the inner face of the vane was often camouflaged. The large glacis engine compartment hatch, painted olive drab on the inside, swings upward and is held open by a stay in the right-hand side. When raised it provides servicing crew with a form of rudimentary shelter against the elements. The engine casing itself is finished in duck egg blue to allow technicians to identify oil leaks, while the bay interior, like the rest of the interior, is painted an eggshell green. The engine can also be accessed internally via a panel to

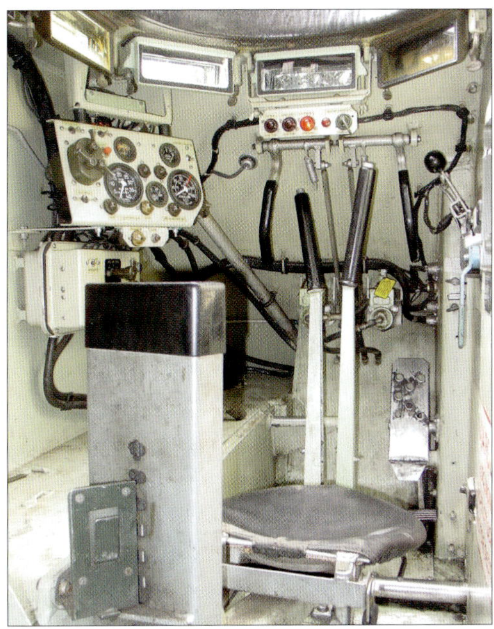

This driver's position is alive with detail. Note the illuminated engine oil warning light. (Chris Conners)

This wonderfully clear shot of an A1 is filled with details, including the 'jump seat'. Note the commander's helmet resting next to the fuel tank, and the clear view into the driver's position. (Chris Conners)

Note the location of the main radio set with the control panel directly below it. (Chris Conners)

This side of the M113 is relatively uncluttered. Note the crew heater in the corner to the right of the commander's position and the opening chain for the cargo hatches. (Chris Conners)

the right of the driver as well as two panels in the troop compartment.

For the interior there are two main variations in terms of finish: the first is pale green or white throughout, the second is white hull walls and floor while the fittings, such as internal fire walls and seating frames are pale green. The rear ramp's inner surface is finished in olive drab, though on some MERDC-finished examples the ramp may also be treated to a dash of camouflage. Radio equipment and heater, situated in the right-hand forward corner of the troop compartment behind the driver, retain their drab finish.

The driving area is spartan, a small instrument panel to the left has various driving control switches including external lighting, heating and bilge pump switches. Directly in front of the driver is the warning light panel. When 'buttoned down', a series of four clear periscopes provide the driver with views directly ahead and to the left. An M19 infrared night-driving periscope is also used, sitting in a special mount set into the driver's hatch and powered by an outlet in the master switch panel below the main instrument panel. When not in use, the M19 is stored to the left of the driver on the hull wall. On the right is a series of levers including hand throttle and ramp controls, while in front are the two accelerator pedals – one for driving with the seat in the raised position and hatch open, the other for when the seat is lowered and the hatch is closed; a harness is also provided for driver safety. As the driver is responsible for the heating, a small box attached to the upper main crossbeam on the left allows for interior climate control. Above and behind the driver is the upper strengthening spar which runs between the vehicle sides.

The troop compartment with the bench seating for five is arranged along the sides

The small rear door is shown in its open position against the ramp. The small rubber box above the jerrycan is the telephone connector. (Chris Conners)

while a folding 'jump seat' is attached to a centrally mounted column, with the commander's collapsible seat attached on the opposite side. To the commander's left is the radio rack and main fire extinguisher, which can be activated externally. When fitted, the small NBC system, consisting of the M8A3 and M13 NBC systems, sits in front of the fire extinguisher.

Directly to his front, mounted above the engine access panels, is the intercom control switch with lighting switches. The commander's cupola is fully rotational, allowing him to aim the mounted .50 cal with ease; a drag brake is fitted to slow rotation with an azimuth lock provided to prevent accidental swing in non-combat situations. The standard commander's cupola is equipped with four M17 periscopes for all-round viewing. Pamphlet bags can be sited on the hull sides and in front of the commander for work tickets and other important documents.

The large roof cargo hatch is opened by a heavy rubber-coated chain that pulls two latches simultaneously and closed by pulling on a single nylon strap; behind this is a small roof-mounted ventilator. Within the troop compartment are 10 roof-mounted grab handles as well as seatbelts (where fitted) to help prevent falls when driving cross-country. All doors and hatches can be secured from the inside by special latches and combat locks to prevent accidental and external opening. On the inner rear starboard wall next to the ramp is the fire extinguisher and the bilge pump outlet pipe, which vents externally. On the port side, on early M113s and A1s, is the large fuel cell, and opposite is the battery box, which moved to the port side of the vehicle in A2 and A3 versions.

The small inset door in the ramp can be held open by a latch; to the right of this, mounted on the outer face of the ramp, are the recovery cables. On the rear crossmember below the ramp is a NATO standard tow hook and electrical connectors for a trailer unit. Either side of the ramp are two jerrycans, the one on the right containing spare fuel, while the jerrycan to the left is the M13 portable decontaminating apparatus. The M13 is used to decontaminate both vehicles and crew-served weapon systems with a calibre greater than .50. The M13 is prefilled with 14 litres of DS2 agent which is enough to decontaminate 1,200 square feet. Its primary use is to remove liquid, blister or nerve agents and some biological agents from exposed surfaces. This is achieved by the crew deploying the self-contained

Left above: The exhaust is the one closest to the camera with the air intake behind it. (Chris Conners)

Left: The M113 is fitted with two bilge vents, a pipe, shown above the rear light, and a flush vent on the port side, parallel to the driver's hatch. (Chris Conners)

hose and wand assembly, which is topped by a stout brush to help remove any decontaminants. The agent is delivered to the brush via an inbuilt handpump, much like a super soaker water pistol.

Rear light units are mounted above the jerrycans, with an external telephone connector sitting inboard of the right rear light. Moving over the top of the M113 are four antenna covers protected by simple blanking plates, which in turn are protected by pronounced antenna guards. Moving forward along the right are two pipes for the internal heater. The one closest to the edge of the hull is the exhaust, while the one to the rear is the air intake. In front of these are two mesh grilles which cover the engine and transmission bay. The inner mesh is the intake grille; underneath sits the air filter and the outside grille covers the exhaust, through which a small exhaust pipe protrudes. Pioneer tools are kept to the rear of the roof, behind the rear hatch aperture, with the refuelling point located in the rear port corner and the bilge pump vent pipe in the rear starboard corner.

In 2007 the T130E1-style track was replaced on M113s operated by the US by T150F track, this change also necessitated the installation of a new-style drive sprocket. The new T150F track features rectangular track shoes as opposed to T-shaped shoes, while the drive sprockets are similar in style to those used on other armoured vehicles such as the M60A3 Patton. Track guards are capable of being folded upward to help with maintenance and in later models a cutout was made in the leading metal attachment point to allow personnel to clamber up.

An evocative shot of an Argentinean Army M113EA on exercise. Note the two-tone khaki and olive drab camouflage. (Argentine Government)

KEY MODELLING ESSENTIALS

The M113 is pretty straightforward in terms of appearance and very little has changed over the years, on the surface at least. Here are some helpful pointers to guide you towards making your authentic build, be it patrolling the rice paddies of Vietnam or the Arctic wastes of Alaska:

- On M113s operating in South East Asia, the side skirts would be removed, as even when folded they would still snag foliage and collect mud and debris.
- Interior space is limited so crews and personnel often hang personal kit and other bagged stores on the front glacis plate and from the sides. Ammunition, ration and specialist equipment boxes are often stored along the roof near the hatch and along the back edge.
- The trim vane, especially on Vietnam-era M113s, was often open to carry extra stores. As this was made from plywood, some wearing of the paint finish soon occurred, revealing the wood underneath.
- If modelling a Vietnam ACAV with the M40 recoilless rifle, remember to remove the commander's front gun shield.
- The A2's key external difference from the A1 is the addition of two large fuel tanks either side of the rear ramp and smoke-grenade launchers on each side of the trim vane of the front glacis plate.
- The M113A3 retains the M113A2's rear fuel tanks, but is also fitted with a swim combing device. There are numerous mounting points for appliqué armour on the hull sides and roof as well as interior sliding spall liners.
- Modern periscopes are given an anti-laser tinting which renders their surface any shade of the red spectrum.
- The interior can be a range of colours from flat white to a pale green.
- If using the MERDC camouflage patterns, pay close attention to the prototypes as the painting of all seven styles was intended to be followed to the letter.
- Most contemporary European and US NATO M113s are finished in the three-colour green, red-brown and black scheme.
- Israeli M113s often have side cages added for extra stowage and adding improvised protection measures such as sandbags. Exhausts are ducted to run down the side of the hull, with the fumes exiting just above the tracks.
- A1 and A2 M113s have tiller bar-type steering while A3s feature a yoke-type steering.
- Contemporary armour upgrades include hardened steel side armour, a slat armour cage bolted to the side armour, and belly anti-mine armour. Other improvements include a turret featuring transparent panels and a bulletproof gun shield similar in design to those fitted on M1165 up-armoured Humvees.
- Later A2 and some A3 models as well as the NASA variant have their glacis-mounted trim vane removed.
- When modelling contemporary M113s, ensure the T150F track and sprockets are mounted rather than the T130E1 style.
- No US operators of the M113 currently use the Type 513B track produced by the German company Diehl, which replaces the previous Type 213 track successfully used by the Bundeswehr and the Australian (ADF) and Danish armies.

M113A3 Body and Dimensions
Basic hull: 5083 aluminium alloy
Width: 2.69m
Total length: 4.86m
Height: 2.20m
Clearance: 410mm
Net weight: 10,832kg
Airdrop weight: 10,037kg
Combat weight 12,3298kg
Max. weight: 14,061kg
Ground pressure: 8.63psi/
    0.6kg/cm²
Fuel capacity: 360l

Engine
Detroit Diesel 6V53T
Cubic capacity: 5.2l
Horsepower: 275hp
Gross horsepower-to-weight ratio:
    20.2hp/ton

Transmission and Braking
Make and model: Allison X200-4
    series (4F2R)
Type: Hydrokinetic
Steering: Yoke-controlled
    hydrostatic
Brake type: Multiple oil-cooled wet
    plate

Running Gear
Suspension: Torsion bar
Shock absorbers: 3 per side

Road wheels: 5 per side, 610mm
    diameter
Track type: T150F steel single pin,
    with detachable rubber pad
Number of shoes: 63 left and 64
    right
Track pitch: 152mm
Track width: 380mm
Wheel travel: 229mm

Electrical Systems
Amperes: 200, 300 optional
Volts, DC: 28
Batteries: 4, type 6TL, 120
    amp-hr, 12v each

Performance
Speed on land: 41mph (66km/h)
Speed in water: 3.6mph (5.8km/h)
Cruising range: 300 miles (483km)
Turning radius: Pivot to infinite
Maximum slope traverse: 60%
Maximum side slope traverse:
    40%
Trench crossing width: 1.68m
Vertical wall climb: 610mm
Emergency braking distance at
    20mph: 12.19m

Armament
1 x .50-cal machine gun w 2,000
    rounds

A dismounted Bulgarian soldier in front of a very tired looking A2 on exercise Combined Resolve II at the Joint Multinational Readiness Centre in Hohenfels, Germany, 20 May 2014. Note the use of the multiple integrated laser engagement system (MILES) on both vehicle and solider and the amber oscillating light on the starboard flank which illuminates when the vehicle is hit. (SSgt. Randy P. Florendo)

In Service & In Action

The M113 exceeded its original design brief, growing into an excellent all-rounder capable of much more than simply the 'battle taxi' duties that were initially envisaged by Continental Army Command (CONARC). From its first contact with the enemy in 1962 in Vietnam it was clear that the M113 had potential beyond its original design specification. Its rugged attributes allowed it to cross the flooded paddy fields and thick jungle with ease, earning it the nickname 'Green Dragon'.

While carried troops were well protected, the shortcomings of the unprotected commander's gun position were soon identified by the Viet Cong (VC). Engagements would see the VC site machine guns to cover the flanks of the line of advance, with coordinated fire converging on the exposed commanders. Another significant issue was the use of the .50 cal. This needed to be 'walked' on to a target, and the power of the firing weapon needed a strong individual to control it. The light build of the AVRN operators, combined with poor training, meant that covering fire was often erratic and fell short of an intended target.

As a result of these experiences and against perceived doctrine of the time, the use of a shield and finally the development of the Armoured Cavalry Assault Vehicle (ACAV) became the in-theatre standard for M113s deployed in the assault role. Not only was the commander protected but the shield also gave the .50 cal a stable firing platform, which allowed the weapon's full lethality – three times greater than the 7.62mm round – to be fully exploited. Shields were also provided for flank-mounted 7.62mm machine guns which were operated via the rear open hatch and acted as flank cover while on the move.

In these situations, infantry would dismount and lead the advance, with cover provided by the M113s in the rear. Given that US tactical doctrine meant that areas would have often been saturated by shells or bombs, the VC and North Vietnamese Army (NVA) troops would take shelter in deep underground tunnels. Once the bombardment had passed, troops would return to prepared fire positions ready to strike at the flank of any advance. The side-mounted machine guns would take care of any such ambushes, and were successful in countering such attempts.

Staff Sergeant Harry F. Mitchell firing the ACAV commander's .50 cal into dense jungle. (US Army)

However, the M113s didn't have it all their own way, and soon the VC and NVA were armed with more sophisticated RPGs and anti-tank devices. These highlighted the weak belly protection of the M113, and initial efforts to mitigate the effect of mines and remotely detonated devices included sandbags laid over the rear area floor and troops riding on the outside of the vehicle. After a few false starts and local efforts, a specifically designed full belly plate of 38mm-thick aluminium armour was introduced in 1970. Another interesting defensive measure, usually taken when

An M113 in ARVN service giving covering fire with its .50 cal. The front bilge pump vent shows signs of use while the recovery cable snaking its way along the port side of the vehicle from front to rear is ready for use. The lack of a commander's gun shield indicates that this is early in the conflict. (US Army)

Members of the mortar platoon, 11th Armoured Cavalry Regiment, fire a 4.2in (106mm) mortar from their M106 at their base camp at Long Giao. Note the commander's ACAV cupola shield. (Pfc A.J. Hand)

ARVN roll in to Cambodia in 1971. Note the lead M113 is fitted with a T50 Gage turret while the side shield for the M60 has been omitted. (US Army)

ACAVs and dismounted infantry advance towards the treeline. Note the rolled mesh fences on the rear and barbed wire hung on the ramps.
(Lt Gen John H. Hay, Jr., US Army)

in a laager position, was the erection of a chain-link fence placed a few feet from the stationary vehicle. This would detonate any incoming B-40 RPG rockets before they could strike the aluminium hull. When not in use, the fence and pickets were rolled up and carried on the glacis plate.

Another variant of the M113 family that was used to great effect in Vietnam was the M163 Vulcan Air Defence System (VADS). With its devastating 20mm M61 Vulcan rotary cannon, VADS were used to engage ground targets as well as provide installation defence from land and air attack. However, their power in the field was also their vulnerability and they would be easily identified and targeted by NVA and VC RPG teams before any other vehicle was attacked.

Meanwhile, the Australians developed their own type of fire-support M113 in the guise of the turreted Saladin fire support vehicle. Given the vulnerability of the M113 to the new generation of RPGs, FSVs were rarely put in situations where any vulnerability could be used against it. They were used primarily as a defensive feature, protecting bases and providing convoy support, though occasionally they would be used for night patrols and snap ambushes.

One interesting event that took place during the 1968 Tet Offensive was the use of an M113 as a rescue vehicle for the US ambassador, Ellsworth Bunker. At 0330 on 30 January 1968, Bunker was woken in his residence by his US Marine guards who had instructions to get him to the US embassy, some four blocks away, as a matter of urgency; there was to be no discussion. Given the urgency and chaos of the situation, Bunker, in his dressing gown and pyjamas, was then thrown into the confined and dark cabin of a waiting M113, which sped him away to the embassy. Given that at that moment it too was under attack, it must have been a nerve-wracking experience. By the end of the Vietnam War a great many M113s were left behind, with some still in Vietnamese service today.

During the immediate post-Vietnam Cold War period, the M113 found itself providing support for US interests globally in a variety of guises. The gaudy graffiti and motifs that had once adorned the flanks of the M113, like the great many conscripts and their chaotic approach to storing equipment, were long gone. The various shades of olive-green finish were replaced by complex MERDC camouflage patterns and disciplined soldiery.

As the second-largest user of the M113, the Israeli Defence Forces' (IDF) first examples were war booty won from Jordanian forces in the Six Day War of 1967. By 1970, new M113A1s were being delivered, seeing action three years later in the Yom Kippur War. Yom Kippur gave the Israelis a sobering taste of the M113's armour when pitted against more sophisticated ground forces than the

Left: M577 ambulance near Xuan Loc, east of Saigon. Note how the trailer has spacers fitted to its axles to ensure its wheels follow the tracks of the towing vehicle rather than making their own and possibly triggering a mine.

Below right: Chaotic scenes unfold as refugees flood past a stalled convoy of M113s, ACAVs and M577s during the Tet Offensive. Note the M40 recoilless rifle on the starboard flank of the ACAV in the middle ground.

Above left: An A1 belonging to the 1st Cavalry Division cruises past with a jubilant occupant. (US Army)

Left: A mechanic cleans his hands while two M113s plough along a mud track on to their next engagement. (US Army)

US faced in Vietnam. During the 1982 Lebanon War, the M113 was once again involved in an urban environment against PLO forces, to which it was more suited. It saw heavy action, although the aluminium armour had a tendency to ignite when hit by some anti-tank weapons. By the time of the siege of Beirut, the M113 was relegated to logistics support and not allowed closer than 100 metres from the front line.

As the 1980s progressed, American foreign policy under the Reagan and Bush administrations was becoming increasing focused on police actions. For example, Panamanian dictator Manuel Noriega was wanted for drug trafficking offences. In the early hours of 20 December 1989, 26,000 troops left their line of departure as part of Operation Just Cause with the aim of apprehending Noriega and installing the democratically elected Guillermo Endara as president.

US forces had planned the operation for just over year and trained for almost six months, so, as expected, all went relatively smoothly. Given that US troops were already stationed in Panama in training facilities such as the jungle training establishments at forts Davies and Sherman, their M113s were deployed. These were used mostly in a force protection and projection role, ready to form roadblocks if needed.

By the time of the 1991 Gulf War, the M113 was in service with most of the friendly forces that had answered the call to liberate Kuwait. As with all friendly forces, the M113 was initially used as a defensive tool, with M113A2s and A3s often being placed in hull-down positions along with M106 and M125 mortar carriers. Other variants used were the M48 and M163 VADS in the air defence roles, the M577 command post, M548 cargo carrier, M981 FIST V artillery support vehicle and the M1098 smoke generator.

Sadly, the A2s did not have a good war and they suffered with issues regarding their inability to keep up with the M2s and M1s, with soldiers being brutally honest about their poor performance. The 1st Infantry Division's after-action report stated that the M113A2 'must be upgraded or replaced' and that the M577 was 'inadequate'. That said, the M113A3 performed well and didn't attract any negative reports.

By the time of the 2003 invasion of Iraq, the M113 was slowly being replaced

Columns of M113s prepare to land in Lebanon during the 1982 war. (Israeli Defence Forces)

Above: Soldiers from the 5th Infantry Division (Mech.) guard the entrance to the Gorgas Army Community Hospital complex during the invasion of Panama. (PH1 (Sw) J. Elliott)

Right: Two M113s from 4th Battalion, 6th Infantry, 5th Infantry Division (Mech.), pass a crowd of demonstrators protesting against the establishment of roadblocks during the invasion of Panama. (PH1 (Sw) J. Elliott)

A Kuwaiti soldier mans his M2 .50-cal machine gun during Operation Desert Shield. (TSgt H.H. Deffner)

Left: An A3 supporting Operation Iraqi Freedom, 2003. (L/Cpl Andrew Young, USMC)

Below: A soldier prepares an M113 ambulance for a convoy during a rapid-deployment exercise on the Johanna Range, Poland. (Sgt Thomas Mort)

on the front line by the M2, and those on the front lines were often configured as A3 ACAVs. Early on the A3 was in the thick of it with combat engineers and medical evacuation teams. One event in April 2003 saw approximately 100 Iraqi soldiers attack Bravo Company of the 11th Engineer Battalion. For an hour and a half, First Sergeant Paul Smith held back the assault with the A3's .50 cal, expending 400 rounds in the process. Smith, later awarded the Medal of Honour, was mortally wounded. As a result, the ACAV gun shield fitting was made available to all M113s in theatre along with a range of other appliqué and slat-type armours.

M113 Variants

Members of the 5th Battalion, 297th National Guard, patrol their area of responsibility during Exercise Brimfrost 1983. (SPC5 Thomas Reilly)

An armoured M58 Smoke Generator Carrier is loaded onto a flatbed trailer by Defense Logistics Agency riggers. (Gs-09 Curtis Lambert)

M1064A3 being reloaded during operation in Iraq, 2003. (Joshua E. Powell, US Army Specialist)

The M113 was exceptionally well designed and as a result showed an extraordinary capability for transformation and adaption. While many overseas users have developed the M113 to meet their own needs, the M113 was developed into an FOV by FMC. Many of these are of interest to the modeller and would sit nicely alongside traditional M113s in a diorama or vignette.

M58 Wolf Smoke Generator Carrier

This is a converted M113 equipped with a M56 smoke generator for laying a smoke screen. The M58 can produce up to 90 minutes of thick, visually impairing smoke, or 30 minutes of infrared-obscuring haze by vaporizing medium-viscosity oil via a specially designed exhaust manifold. The smoke is then directed to the rear of the vehicle and leaves via an aperture situated on the vehicle's rear right flank.

M106, M125 & M1064 Self-propelled Mortar Carriers

The standard mortar-carrier version carries a turntable-mounted M30 107mm mortar in the rear cargo bay, protected by a three-part circular hatch. A base plate is mounted on the left flank of the hull, allowing the mortar to be used in a dismounted role. The M125 carries the M29 81mm mortar, which is able to bring down rounds much closer to the vehicle to help regain the advantage after an ambush. The US Army now uses the M1064A3, which carries the larger M121 120mm mortar and which saw extensive use in Iraq.

M113 VISMOD

The Visual Modification (VISMOD) versions of the M113 have significant structural changes or paint finishes that change their overall appearance. These turn the standard vehicle into a close replica of a Soviet BMP 1. The vehicle is equipped with a fake turret, reshaped glacis plate and rear ramp. Also called the M113 OPFOR Surrogate Vehicle (OSV), these vehicles are used for more realistic training.

M113A4 Armoured Medical Evacuation Vehicle

The M113A4 Armoured Medical Evacuation Vehicle (AMEV) is specifically modified and equipped for use as an armoured ambulance, replacing earlier M113s that fulfilled a basic medical evacuation by providing medical services with a bespoke vehicle. It provides the on-board medic with room to monitor wounded personnel but has enhanced storage for equipment as well as improvements to capabilities. These

Left: VISMOD in action. (Maj Wayne Clyne)

Below: An M132 Flamethrower on display at the War Remnants Museum, Ho Chi Minh City, Vietnam.

include an on-board oxygen production unit, an NBC over-pressure filtration system, improved interior lighting, a medical suction system and engine noise reduction measures. An improved litter configuration is also included, allowing for the accommodation of either four litter cases or eight ambulatory patients. As with all A4 standard M113s, the AMEV is equipped with the RISE power package to give it the capability of maintaining a presence with front line units.

M132 Flamethrower

Armed with a turret-mounted M10-8 flamethrower and coaxial 7.62mm M73 machine gun, the M132 saw extensive use in Vietnam. The 757l fuel load was carried in four spherical 189l fuel tanks and fed to the M10-8 by an M10 fuel and pressure unit housed in the stripped-out passenger compartment. The M132 had 32 seconds of firing with a range of up to 170m.

M150 Tow Carrier

The anti-tank guided missile (ATGM) variant of the M113 is equipped with a single TOW missile launcher sited in front of the rear hatch, with missiles stowed internally.

M163 Vulcan Air Defense System (VADS)

The M163 is an SPAAG version (self-propelled anti-aircraft, gun) armed with a 20mm M168 Vulcan autocannon which is guided by the AN/VPS-2 range-only radar and M61 optical lead-calculating sight. The VADS has rapid-fire capabilities and is accurate to two miles. It could also be used against land targets, as in Vietnam.

M577 Command Post & M1068 Command Post System (SICPS)

The M577 Command Post features a raised after section, housing all the equipment that a command post would require: a folding map table, radios, an integrated cabin heater, as well as a portable 28v generator. The hull roof has been raised by 650mm, along with twin 60-gal fuel tanks

and a hand-cranked 10m antenna mast. The working area can also be extended rearward by the addition of a tent. M577s in medical use were primarily for triage and occasionally treatment, as the taller rear compartment gave more room to work, and the generator allowed for a wider variety of medical equipment to be used. A recent sub-variant is the M1068 Standard Integrated Command Post System Carrier (SIPSC), which also carries the Army Tactical Command and Control System (ATCCS). Some have been fitted with the RISE power pack, giving those versions the M1068A3 designation.

An M150 during the joint South Korea/US Exercise Team Spirit 1984. (APC SPC4 Long)

Crewmen of the 24th Infantry Division with their M163 Vulcan self-propelled anti-aircraft gun stand ready during an exercise at the National Training Centre, Fort Irwin, California. Note the way kip mats have been stowed. (US Army)

Dutch M577 Pantser Rups-Commando (PRCO) Command Post is awash with detail to whet the appetite of any modeller. (Alf van Beem)

An M901 Improved TOW Vehicle passes down a road in the Laubach Wald area during the Confident Enterprise phase of Reforger/Autumn Forge 1983. (CMSgt Don Sutherland, US Air Force)

A great study of an M579 in a wintry setting. (Ministry of National Defence Republic of Lithuania)

M579 Fitter Repair Vehicle

The M579 is fully capable of supporting field and engineering repairs to a range of military vehicles. Mounted on the left rear of the roof is a HIAB model 173 hydraulic crane controlled from the driver's compartment. The crane is capable of lifting 1,660kg at 3.3m reach on the hook at the tip of the boom, or 3,085kg at 1.7m on the intermediate hook. A large roof hatch gives access to the rear cargo compartment inside the hull and, by using the crane, a complete engine and transmission pack can be removed. The M579 did not enter US service, but has been widely exported.

M806 Armoured Recovery Vehicle

The M806 features an internal winch and two large earth anchors mounted either side of the rear hull. During operations the ground anchors are folded down, and a cross-brace spade section, which is carried on the roof of the unit when not in use, is placed between them. The M806 is then reversed to raise its rear off the ground, while simultaneously allowing the ground anchors and spade the opportunity to dig in and provide a steady winching platform. Once winching begins, a collapsible steel grille is raised in front of the winch to provide protection for the operator should the cable break. The M806 did not enter US service, but has been widely exported.

M901 Improved TOW Vehicle

The M901 Improved TOW Vehicle (ITV) was designed to carry dual M220 TOW launchers. The launchers are fitted to a hydraulically and electrically powered 'Hammerhead' turret, attached to a modified M27 cupola. The launcher has day and night target tracking and acquisition systems and provides the ITV with a 360° firing coverage and +35° to −30° degrees elevation. Capable of firing two missiles before having to reload, which is performed by tilting the launching apparatus rearward so the crew can access the turret via carrier's rear roof hatch to reload from the 10-round missile rack. When stowed, the turret is aimed down and positioned to the rear of the vehicle. The ITV also has the capability to carry the tripod-mounted M220-series TOW weapon system, that can be deployed if necessary.

M981 Fire Support Team Vehicle

The M981 Fire Support Team Vehicle (FISTV) is used by artillery observer teams and Combat Observation and Lasing Teams (COLTs) in mechanized units. Based on the M901 to make it look less obvious on the battlefield, the FISTV identifies targets, sending relevant descriptions and locations on to the Fire Direction Centre. The principal equipment on the FISTV is the Ground/Vehicular Laser Locator Designator (G/VLLD) which is mounted in the adopted 'Hammerhead' mount. The G/VLLD is capable of obtaining precise range information from an identified target that has been laser-tagged. When combined with directional control from a gyroscopic inertial navigation system and accurate vehicle location from GPS, the system produces the precise target coordinates. For full connectivity with artillery and the relevant unit chains of command, the M981 is fitted with four Single Channel Ground and Airborne Radio Systems (SINCGARS).

M1059 Lynx Smoke Generator Carrier

The M1059 carries an M157 smoke-generating set which is fed by a 450l fog oil tank with an M54 smoke generator mounted either side of the vehicle roof, protected by armour shields. The generators vaporize the fog oil with heat produced from a pulse jet engine, with the oil condensing once it has dispensed, forming a large white cloud. The fog oil capacity is enough to provide 120 minutes of operation.

YPR-765 Armoured Infantry Fighting Vehicle (AIFV)

Based on the M113A1 and part-developed from the MICV-65 programme, the YPR-765 was a seriously modified M113 with a redesigned hull, featuring an enclosed turret and firing ports, enabling mounted infantry to fire from within the vehicle. Later designated the AIFV (Armoured Infantry Fighting Vehicle), the Dutch were the first to order 880 units, in 1975. In total they ordered 1,264, making a further 815 under licence. During their deployment in Afghanistan, several Dutch AIFVs were fitted with additional armour. Other users included the Philippines, Malaysia, Belgium and Turkey. The Dutch also operate the PRI (Pantser Rups Infanterie) version armed with a 25mm KBA-B02 cannon and a coaxial 7.62mm FN MAG in an EWS turret (enclosed weapon station). Other versions include the YPR-765 prrdr (Pantser Rups Radar) equipped with a ZB-298 battlefield surveillance radar, and the TOW-armed YPR-765 PRAT (Pantser Rups Anti-Tank).

M113 Chassis-based variants

These modified versions of the M113 chassis are all based in the M548 Cargo Carrier. FMC were keen to exploit the chassis' adaptability and produced a range of vehicles to operate behind the front line, providing logistical and indirect fire support.

Members of the 1/41st Field Artillery Battalion observing fire from the rear of their M981A3 Fire Support Team Vehicle (FIST-V). (Don Teft)

An M1059 lays down a wall of smoke during the combined Exercises Reception, Staging, Onward Movement, and Integration/Foal Eagle 2002 held in South Korea. (Jo2(Sw) Stacy Young, USN)

Dutch troops from 2 Platoon, E Company, Battle Group 7, Task Force Uruzgan prepare to move toward Mirabad, Afghanistan 2008. (Mass Communication Specialist 1st Class John Collins, US Navy)

M548

The M548A3 is designed specifically for cargo carrying, capable of transporting a six-tonne payload and a crew of four. Its primary function is to supply artillery units with ammunition. The large rear cargo area is readily accessed for ease of unloading. For self-defence the M548 can carry either a 7.62mm or .50 cal mounted over the cab and accessed from a hatch in the cab roof. Like the M113, the M548 is fully air-transportable.

M688 Carrier Guided Missile (Lance)

The M688 carries a maximum of two MGM-52 Lance tactical surface-to-surface missiles that can be fitted with either a nuclear or a conventional warhead with a maximum operational range of 120km. The M688 is equipped with a crane to lift the rockets onto the M752 launch vehicle.

M727 Guided Missile Carrier (Hawk)

The M727 is a tracked carrier vehicle designed to transport the Hawk guided missile system developed by BAe Corporation as a medium-range, guided

An immaculate M548 in British desert colours. (Simon Quinton)

M727 Guided Missile Equipment Carrier (Hawk) at Muzeyon Heyl ha-Avir, Hatzerim, Israel.

A M730 Guided Missile (Chaparral) Taiwanese M730A1 on display at Taiwan Air Force Base, Miroko Sunn.

anti-aircraft missile system for the United States Army. The M727's missile system is the Raytheon MIM-23 Hawk, a medium-range, radar-guided surface-to-air guided missile. Three of these large missiles are carried while a dedicated missile loading tractor, the M501, is on hand to reload missiles onto the rear-mounted rotating turret system. The M727 has a range of unique safety features: the rear of the cab and engine compartment is covered by a large blast shield while the suspension can be locked to stabilize the M727 during loading and firing. A roll-over protective structure (ROPS) was added to the cabs of M727s deployed in Europe. A 60Kw generator is also carried and this powers the missile system. Unlike the M548, the M727 missile carrier is not amphibious.

M48 (M730) Guided Missile (Chaparral)

The M48 Chaparral Intercept-Aerial Guided Missile System is composed of a fully rotational M54 launching station mounted on the rear flatbed of the M730 carrier. The system carries four AIM-9 Sidewinder missiles, with a further eight stored below the launcher with fins and wings removed. The gunner is seated within the launch station with the missiles either side of him, aiming with a simple reflex sight, though a FLIR unit is also provided for all-weather/ night capability. The M48 also features an auxiliary power unit to run the system while a cryonic air cooler provides the missile seekers with the necessary cooling.

M752 Missile Launcher (Lance)

The M752 'Lance' missile system is an all-in-one launch and resupply vehicle capable of carrying the Ling-Temco-Vought (LTV) MGM-52 Lance. The Lance can be armed with a 100Kt nuclear warhead as well as conventional anti-tank and anti-fortification warheads. It is powered by a liquid-propellant rocket motor that can generate speeds in excess of Mach 3 and carry the payload 120km, guided by an inertial guidance system. Along with the M688 resupply vehicle, a single M752 can launch three missiles in field conditions. The M752 was produced and operated by the United States, Great Britain, Belgium, Israel, Italy, West Germany and the Netherlands.

M1108 Universal Carrier

The XM1108 is based on a modified M113A4 using the hull as a carrier that is capable of carrying a 7-tonne load on a large shallow-sided flatbed. The M1108 utilizes the armoured cabin of the M993 Multiple Launch Rocket System (MLRS) carrier to protect the crew from small-arms fire.

RCM 748 Tracked Rapier

The M548-based Tracked Rapier system was developed by the British Aircraft Corporation (BAC) to protect armoured battle groups from air attack. To enable this, BAC attached a completely redesigned missile-launching system that could be armed with eight Rapier surface-to-air missiles. The specially designed armoured cabin housed all the relevant missile control mechanisms and was provided with climate control as well as full NBC protection. Optical tracking of target was done via an optical tracker that could be elevated through the roof, and the tactical controller was also equipped with a special helmet-mounted sight allowing him to visually track the target. Fully air-portable, the RCM 748 could be made ready to fire in 30 seconds. Initial RCM 748s had no space for the Marconi DN 181 'Blindfire' radar on the launcher vehicle, so this is either towed or carried on a separate, modified M548/RCM748. The second vehicle provided the launcher with the necessary fire-control information via connective wires that fed data to the control system in the firing unit. As this took time to connect and set up, RCM 748s were upgraded with a thermal-imaging enhanced tracker, which eliminated the 'Blindfire' radar unit. The RCM 748 was accompanied into the field by a modified M548 Missile Resupply Vehicle, a relief crew and additional field kit, rations and water. A further M548 was configured as an REME Forward Area Support team with the necessary test facilities and spares.

SPECIAL VARIANTS

Vietnam Gun-Truck Hybrid

The Gun-Truck Hybrid utilized damaged M113s that were mounted on to the large cargo bed of the powerful M54 6x6 5-tonne truck. The M113 hull gave the troops of the Transportation Corps the protection they needed as they accompanied the large convoys that snaked across Vietnam supplying friendly forces. Although well-armed and aggressive-looking, these trucks were purely defensive. Painted in a range of colours including gloss and satin black, the M113s were often adorned with graffiti, making the Gun-Truck Hybrids among the most aggressive-looking, garish and eye-catching M113s in Vietnam.

NASA

An M113 was kept at the foot of NASA's launchpads in case an emergency exit was needed. Every astronaut was trained to drive the vehicle before launch, and this seems to have been a favoured activity of the intense NASA astronaut training programme. These unique M113s were often 'tagged' with mission stickers placed on the front or rear of the body. They were finished in lime yellow with a white waistband, and large red numbers on all sides of the hull.

Law Enforcement

Several law enforcement agencies use the M113 in a variety of roles, from the original APC role as a SWAT support vehicle, to

The M752 is more of a museum piece than a serious bit of hardware. (Alf van Beem)

The RCM 748 gave battle groups the mobile top cover they would have needed should the Cold War have ever heated up. (Simon Quinton)

Captain George Hoggard, trainer with the Kennedy Space Center Fire Department, oversees STS-106 Commander Terrence W. Wilcutt as he practises driving the M113 that is part of emergency egress training. All of NASA's M113s were finished in lime green. Note the mission stickers on the white stripe around the glacis plate. (2000, NASA)

command and control or armoured rescue vehicles. These would be an interesting choice of the M113 to model and are finished with a range of gloss liveries, from navy blue to white, with relevant details.

M106A1 Mortar Carrier Operation Attleboro Phase VI

This M106 mortar track belongs to the 2nd Battalion 22nd Infantry (Triple Deuce) Regiment, operating as part of the 2nd Brigade Task Force during Operation Attleboro, 13 November 1966 near the Cambodian/South Vietnam border. The operation was the first US Army Seek and Destroy mission in Vietnam and featured no less than four US Army divisions. Launched on 14 September the operation would finally cease on 25 November. The role of the M106 was to provide indirect fire support to the infantry of the 2nd Battalion as they moved forwards. Being mounted they were able to move quickly and keep pace with advancing infantry. M113s and M106s at this early state of the Vietnam conflict were well kept and relatively free of individual markings and graffiti.

M113A1 Reforger MERDC Colour Scheme

Exercise Campaign Reforger (Return of Forces to Germany) was an annual NATO exercise held during the Cold War. The intent was to ensure NATO, particularly the US, had the ability to quickly deploy forces to West Germany in the event of a conflict with Warsaw Pact forces. This US-based M113A1 belongs to 1st Battalion, 4th Infantry Regiment (Mech), 1st Cavalry Division, who were operating out of Kaiserslautern for the duration of Reforger 1983.

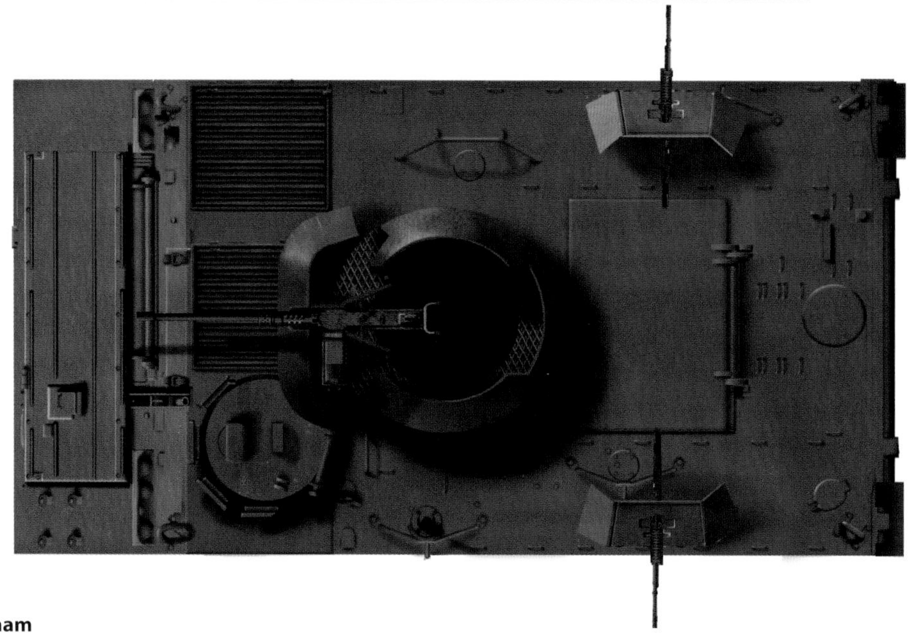

M113 ACAV Vietnam

The ACAV was the first major variant of the M113 to be developed. Learning lessons from the Army of Vietnam (ARVN) the US developed the Armoured Cavalry Assault Vehicle (ACAV). The ACAV was a vital piece of support armour that was able to provide fearsome firepower and excellent manoeuvrability. In the field the ACAV's were soon adorned with a host of personal markings, cartoon characters and graffiti. As the war progressed the markings would become more ornate, offensive and decorative. The vehicles would be covered with personal and mission-critical equipment such as rolls of fencing, ammunition boxes as well as deckchairs and large umbrellas.

M113A3 South Dakota National Guard

200th Engineering Company South Dakota National Guard were based at Camp Warhorse during Operation Iraqi Freedom from April 2003 to March 2004. During their time in theatre the 200th completed a range of tasks including bridge building, the unit's primary role. The 200th received the Army Valorous Unit Award upon their return home in recognition of their work during a tour which often saw the unit under fire. The 200th went to Iraq with a huge amount of operational experience including two Vietnam veterans, three Desert Storm veterans and one Bosnia and Herzegovina veteran. Vehicles often carried insulated boxes filled with water bottles and stowed on top of vehicles to save precious space.

NASA M113A1

Cape Canaveral, Florida. From the start of the Apollo missions until 2014 NASA kept a fleet of four M113 A1s as escape and fire-and-rescue vehicles. At every launch the M113s would be deployed thus: two containing NASA firefighters in their familiar silver suits parked and ready less than a mile from the launch site, and a single M113 kept ready for action next to the astronauts' evacuation bunker, buried 12m underneath the launch pad. Finished in firefighting luminous green, a colour used by US military specification firefighting appliances, with a horizontal reflective stripe and large reference number. All astronauts were taught to drive the M113 and a common practice among crews is to add mission stickers to the front glacis plate or hull rear.

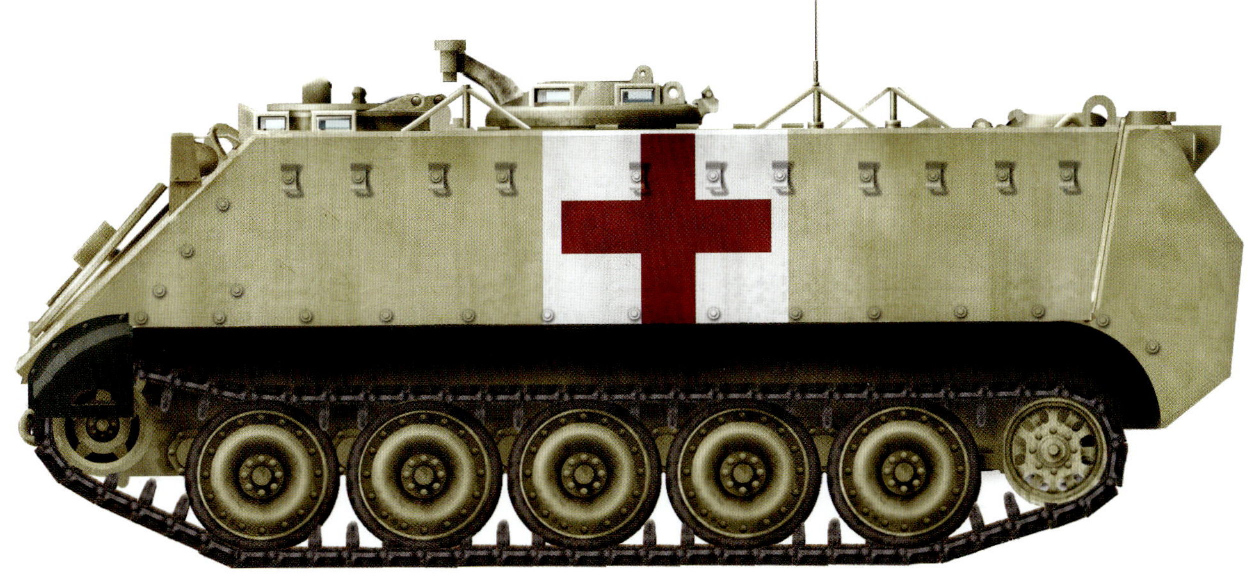

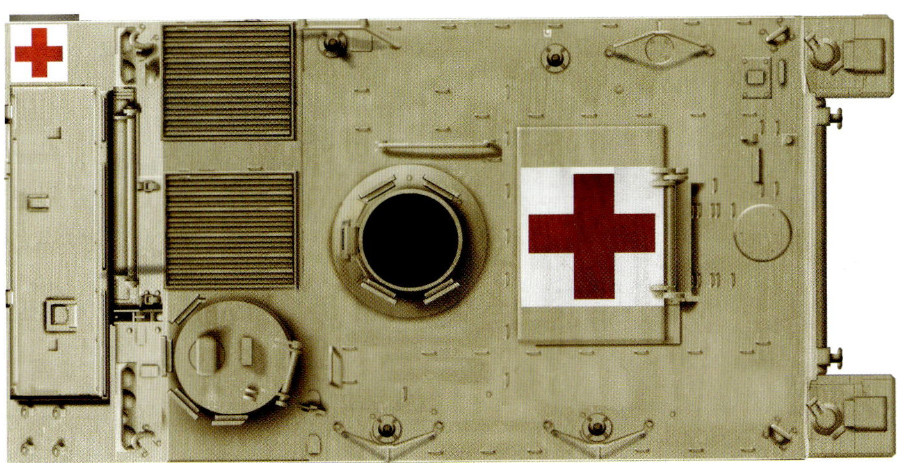

M113A3 Armoured Medical Evacuation Vehicle
Company C ('Charlie Med'), 64th Brigade Support Battalion, 3rd Armoured Brigade Combat Team, 4th Infantry Division, Hohenfels Training Area, Germany, 2017. Deployed as part of the US contingent for Exercise Combined Resolve VIII, which included more than 3,400 participants from ten nations uniting for a for a two-week combat training centre exercise, Charlie Med provided vital medical support to exercising troops in the field. The exercise was designed to give units one last shakedown and training opportunity before returning to the continental United States. As the exercises are seen as shakedowns personal discipline is tight and vehicles are rarely festooned with the personal equipment often associated with deployed vehicles.

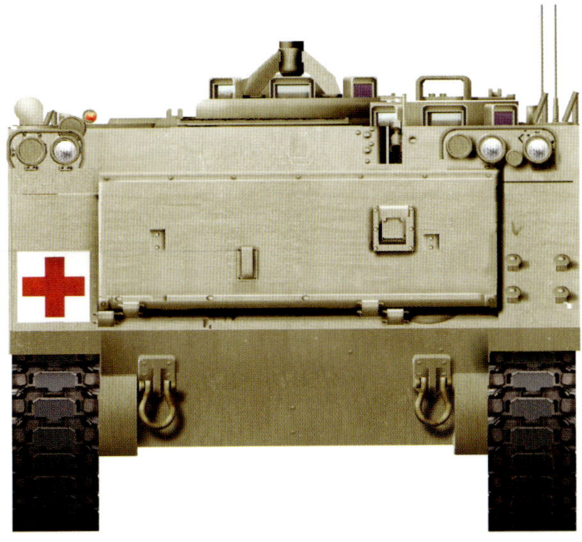

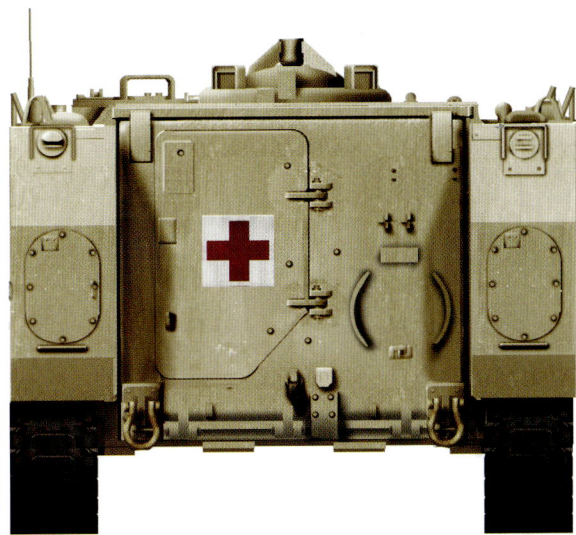

Republic of Korea, Tiger Division, Vietnam

The Republic of South Korea operated the M113 and M113 ACAV as part of their contribution to the war in Vietnam. Known as 'The Tigers', the Capital Mechanized Infantry Division operated in central South Vietnam protecting lines of communication, including Route 1 and 19. The Tigers gained a reputation for their uncanny ability to locate enemy troops and their innate professionalism in planning and executing operations. The M113s used by 'The Tigers' all featured a large roaring tiger's head painted onto the front glacis plate. The M113's featured a tricolour camouflage of an Olive Green base coat over painted with a soft edged matt black pattern which would have small areas of matt blue painted onto it.

Israeli Defence Forces Nagmash
Since 1973, the M113 has been the main APC in Israeli Defence Force service with over 6,000 variants in use by the mid-1990s. The Israeli Defence Forces introduced many improvements to the basic design (such as taking the main fuel tank out of the vehicle) and to the armour as a result of lessons learned in the Yom Kippur and Lebanon wars. The side rails on the flanks are for equipment stowage which were often utilized to stow sandbags which acted as additional armour for those M113s on patrol along the border areas. The exhaust is routed thought a u-pipe bend and exits along the side of the vehicle just above the tracks.

M113A1 MVR

B Squadron, 2nd Cavalry Regiment, Australia

1/35 Scale

Brian Richardson

The MRV (Medium Reconnaissance Vehicle) variant of the M113 family replaced the Saladin-turreted FSV (Fire Support Vehicle) in the Australian Army in the early 1980s and 48 were built. It was fitted with a Scorpion CVR(T) turret equipped with the same 76mm gun as its predecessor and had a much improved fire-control system. It was also equipped with floatation tanks to cope with the extra weight of the turret to maintain its swimming capability. These have all been withdrawn from service and placed in reserve. The AFV Club kitted this unique Australian AFV in 1999 and they were initially known as FSVs during the development phase. Later they were designated as MRVs when its role had changed. This build is a mix of re-boxed Academy and new AFV Club parts for the turret; it still builds into a respectable model. Some homemade bed rolls have been added as well as wire tie-down loops, wire mesh over the engine grills and a tissue dust cover for the main gun. Tamiya acrylics were used with some oils and pastels for weathering. The model is based on M113A1 MRVs that served with B Squadron, 2nd Cavalry Regiment during exercise Northern Predator in and around the Mount Bundey Military Training Area southeast of Darwin, Northern Territory, Australia in late 1994.

M113A1 MVR
Australian Army, 1990s
1/35 Scale
Federico Collada

This model is a kit cross of re-boxed AFV Club parts and new Academy parts with the Scorpion turret. Close attention must be paid to the mounting of the turret. The general quality of the model is good although it can be improved in places. The assembly is fairly simple and the instruction manual is very clear. To carry out the detailing work, it will be essential to have good reference material for the vehicle in question, since both the M113 hull and the Scorpion turret differ from the originals. The detailing itself is nothing to write home about, I have not had to resort to photo-etched parts or conversion kits. A bit of brass, plastic sheet, some tubes, putty, a little wire and an iron were enough, not to mention rivets and a mini-drill.

The entire model was first painted khaki, applying lights and leftovers. The green spots were then added without using masks so that the edge was diffused. After giving the consequent lights and shadows the black spots were added which were lightened a little with green and grey to give the lights.

After painting the details, lights, exhausts, visors etc., the whole vehicle was lightly powdered (more on the underbody, wheels and chains), and finally a little graphite to reveal the metal. The black in the colour pattern is lightened with a mixture of black, medium grey and drab khaki. For green spots use medium green, olive green for shadows and inner green for highlights.

The barrel sleeve is made with modelling putty which was shaped with a toothpick. The tapes are made of very thin plastic and the buckles of residue. The caps of the smoke canisters are made of plastic rod turned with the mini-drill.

After placing the decals the process of weathering of the paint began. Trying not to give the impression of a tank in combat but of one on manoeuvres, a less severe approach was taken. Then scratches, chips, melts, filters and some metal screws (they are usually seen when the originals are replaced) finished the job.

M113A1

11th Cavalry, 'Blackhorse Regiment', Operation Fargo, Long Binh, Vietnam 1967

1/35 Scale
Ben Skipper

Tamiya's venerable M113 kit has been used to portray a 4th Squadron, 11th Cavalry Support A1. The 11th used a variety of M113s to support their ongoing mission. These worked alongside the regiment's M109, M551s and M48. The 11th were a self-contained battle group, which was able to field airborne troops alongside armour and mechanized infantry. The kit is showing its age alongside more contemporary offerings, but that said, with some Eduard etch (Set 35406), Black Dog and Legend resin Vietnam accessories and Master Club tracks (MTL35113) it can really come to life. Rather than build the kit and then add the PE, the latter was added first, adhering delicate items with Gorilla superglue, then built. This saved a huge amount of time. The assembly could be broken down into simple stages that, once painted, literally fell together.

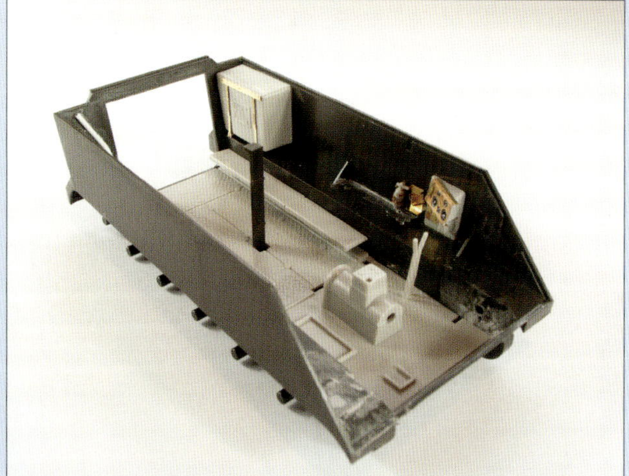

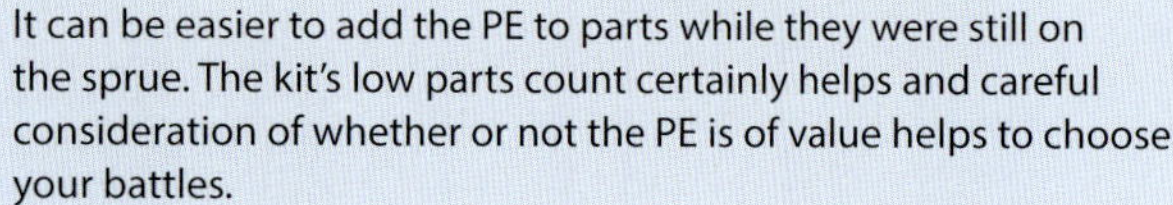

It can be easier to add the PE to parts while they were still on the sprue. The kit's low parts count certainly helps and careful consideration of whether or not the PE is of value helps to choose your battles.

The tracks were tricky, but, by bringing them together and using a sewing pin as hold while grappling with the small pins, runs of ten can be made. Once built they were given a light overspray of matt black and the track pads were then glued into position.

The colour finish is Duck Egg Green for the interior (Val71009) with a Forest Green pre-shade (AK4013) and Colours Olive Drab No31 (AK4215) for the exterior with a black green pre-shade (TamXF27). Details were picked out in a range of colours and a gloss varnish (Val70522) was airbrushed over the whole model ready for decals (Echelon Fine Decals D356168 11-4 Cav M113A1 in Vietnam).

The Master Club tracks vs the kit-supplied vinyl tracks are far better in terms of quality. The drive sprockets do need to be changed and thankfully the AFV Club set supplied in AF35306 outer matched the kit inners, which received some minor surgery. The final piece of PE to go in was the floor. Going for it makes all the difference.

The interior is now built up. The smaller dials on the driver's instrument panel were painted with a spot of paint on the end of cocktail stick. On the rear bulkhead is the added fire extinguisher and bilge pump pipe. As APCs get extremely dirty and dusty once out in the field, one can go to town on the weathering. Crushed red-brown pastel was applied to the chequer plate and ramp floors before receiving a wash of homemade solution. The interior has the wash applied vertically on the side and in the engine bay, while the engine received a couple of coats before disappearing from view.

The final model had a few details added, including food and water containers, commander's boonie hat and portable transistor set. The radio antennas were florist's wire with nylon thread. The interior was fitted with a kitbag and small day sack for the crew. The .50cal was taken from another kit to replace the simple version that came with the original. The brass rounds have been painted black and a coloured artist's pencil has highlighted the raised elements. The hull received some wear marks in white and silver in a few places but overall the paintwork damage is minimal.

M113A1 FSV

3rd Cavalry Regiment, Royal Australian Armoured Corps, Vietnam 1971

1/35 Scale
Brian Richardson

This model is Tamiya's rendition of the M113A1 FSV in Australian service. The vehicle came about to fill a requirement – gained from experience in the war in South Vietnam – to add fire support to the cavalry regiments equipped with M113A1 Armoured Personnel Carriers. Fifteen Saladin armoured cars were being phased out of service and it was decided to mate the turrets to diesel-powered M113A1s purchased specifically for the conversion. The work was completed at 4 Base Workshop Bandiana Victoria in 1970. They could also be upgraded with bolt-on belly armour and additional 20mm armour plate welded under the sponsons above the first three road wheels for anti-mine protection. Mines had taken a heavy toll on the aluminium hulls of the M113s and their crews. Eight of the 15 FSVs served in Vietnam late 1971 in 3rd Cavalry Regiment, doing road and area patrols, as well as occasionally in convoy escort support missions. All vehicles were returned on Australia's withdrawal from the conflict and served until 1980 when they were replaced by the Scorpion-turreted FSV, later renamed the MRV. Tamiya's kit is an oldie dating back to 1979 and is still available. This model represents Bewitched, one of the eight FSVs sent to Vietnam. The O/D was mixed from Tamiya acrylics XF-62 Olive Drab and XF-49 Khaki. Mouse House decals completed the markings and their sheet, MAD608, provides for all eight FSVs that went to Vietnam.

The driver and commander figures are by Call Sign Models and are made specifically for Australian armoured vehicles.

Note the exhaust's handle that allowed the pipe to be turned to the rear to allow a wading screen to be fitted. With the extra weight of the turret FSVs had much less freeboard and the screen reduced the risk of water entering the engine compartment.

Much of the added detail can be seen here which more accurately represents the real thing, including Armour Bits roof, Eduard leaf screens, tie downs and of course lots of copper wire and plastic card.

Note the trim vane extension included with the Armour Bits set and the belly armour scratched from 1mm card and bolted in place with Meng nuts.

Extra mud and dust has been added to the roof, where the crew's boots would have rubbed, using ground pastels fixed with thinners.

AFV Club M113 indy track links replace the Tamiya vinyls for a more realistic appearance. There are enough spares to add extra links in front of the driver's position.

New hinges have been 'welded' in with Squadron green putty and two Armour Bits jerry can racks have been filled with Italeri items tied down with straps from Tamiya tape.

Smoke grenade launchers were removed soon after arrival in SVN to prevent them being damaged by moving through thick brush and to remove the risk of being ignited by enemy fire.

Each link has a sink mark that was filled with Mr Surfacer, a tedious job but in the end worth the effort.

Washes of Humbrol black enamel fill in the tracks and tyres after the O/D is applied

Modelling the M113

Extremely popular and well served by model manufacturers, the M113 has been the subject of a huge range of kits in all scales. All have their merits with great potential to add multi-media detailing and conversion parts. Kits can also be incorporated into both small vignettes and large scale dioramas with other genres of model making. As new models are always being produced this list is purely contemporaneous and features manufactures that are still trading at the time of writing.

Model Kits of M113

Dragon have released two versions of their popular Panzer Korps 1/144 combos featuring the M113. The first is a Gulf-themed combo (14039) featuring an M113A3 and M3A2, whilst the second features a Bundeswehr Leopard 2A6 and M113A3 (14027). The kits are multi part, moulded in heavy plastic and include simple detailing for engine grills and crew loads which can be added at the modeller's discretion.

MR Modellbau produce a wide range of 1/87 resin M113's which include Swiss (87091), Danish (87134) and Israeli (87062) multi-part resin kits. They also produce conversion and detailing kits for the 1/87 range including interior fittings (87064) and a dozer blade (87013). As well as the 1/87 kits and conversions *MR Modellbau* have produced detailing kits for 1/35 modellers with an interest in European M113s, castings are sharp, and the subject matter has been well researched. These have been designed to be used with both AFV Club and Tamiya M113s and include a Danish Army armour upgrade set (35425), GE EFT A0 artillery computer (35294) and a Bundeswehr equipment set (1995 – 2004) for the M113 A1G.

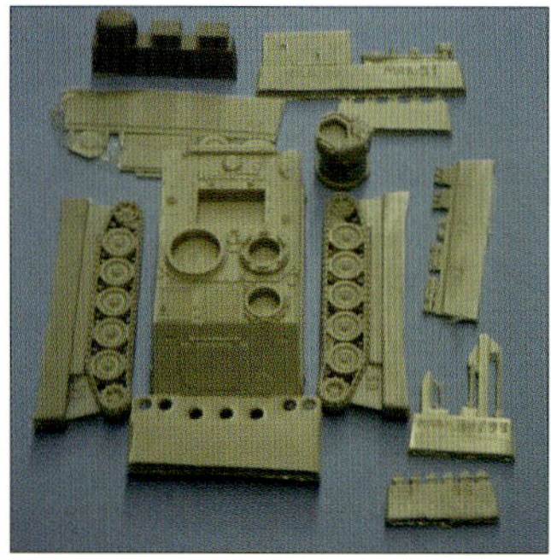

MR Swiss M113.

Arsenal Green Archer.

Another German-based manufacturer of 1/87 M113 kits is *ArsenalM*. Their models are a mix of M113s in various guises and include a Bundeswehr Green Archer mortar-locating radar, a Davy Crockett projectile conversion kit and the NASA rescue M113.

Italian manufacturer *Brach Model* have produced an interesting resin models of the M113 in 1/72 including the Italian VCC-1 (BM-7212), which is very similar in appearance to the AIFV version of the M113.

Continuing with the 1/72 scale offerings, *Hobby Den Resins* of Ireland have produced a wonderful range of resin and white metal kits, these include Bundeswehr M113G mortar and Milan carriers (HD102 and HD87). The kits are single-piece mouldings for the bodies with hatches and cupolas cast separately. The details are a touch soft, but with some judicious knife work and careful painting these little models will really stand out.

French manufacturer *Model Miniature* has produced resin kits of two very interesting Pakistani versions of the M113; the first is the Talha six-wheeled APC (MM-R197) and the Al Qaswa cargo carrier (MM-R196). Both are beautifully sculpted with a very small parts count, two and three respectively. In service with the Iraqi Army, these would make great editions to a contemporary diorama. *Model Miniature* has also produced some generic tracks (MM-R078) for the standard five wheeled M113.

Modell Trans Modelbau have produced resin upgrades and conversions sets for *Italeri* and *Trumpeter* 1/72 M113's as well as a splendidly observed multi-part resin kits of the Lynx reconnaissance vehicle (MT72167) and the Zelda II (MT72235). Conversions include the M579 Fitter Vehicle (MT72141) for Trumpeters offering and replacement tracks and wheels for the *Italeri* M113 (MT72111). Some of the *Modell Trans Modelbau* have come from the now defunct Cromwell Models range including the Zelda II with Toga armour.

In the plastic model kit world *Italeri*, *Trumpeter* and *S-Model* have all produced some excellent and interesting 1/72 kits for the modeller. *Italeri* have bought the old ESCI moulds of the M113 family and from these produced the M106 mortar carrier (7069), and the M163 Vulcan (7066). Moulded in khaki plastic across two spures, the details are pretty standard for the scale. Sadly the lack of a driver's position is disappointing and the inclusion of plastic rather than vinyl tracks may make build tricky for the novice. Instructions are clear and the decals allow for four differing versions to be built, including a Vietnam version.

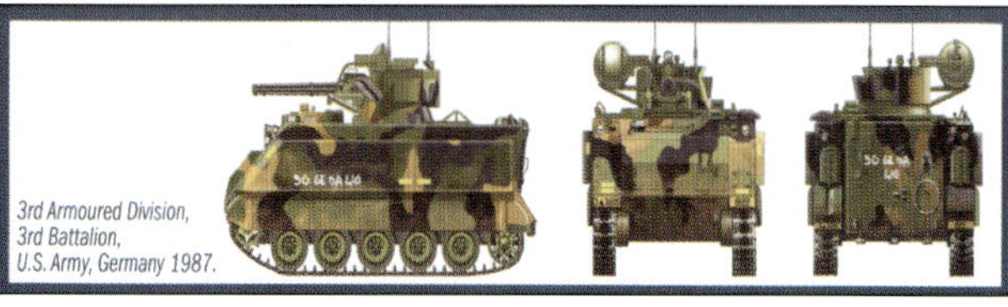

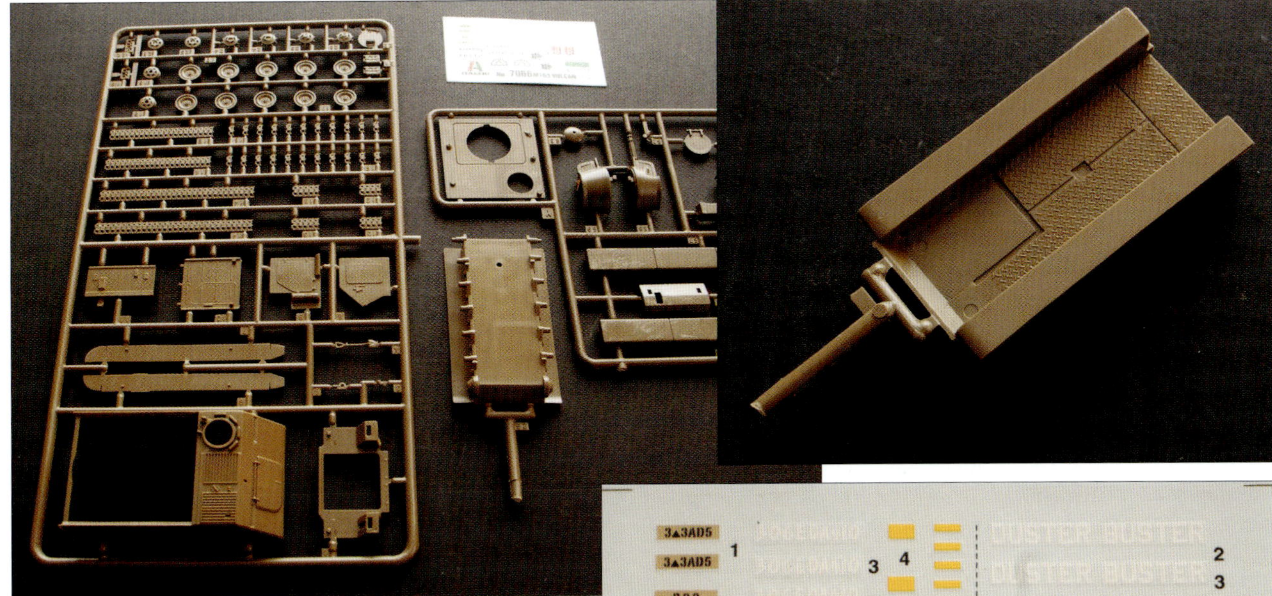

Trumpeter offers four versions of the M113; the ACAV (07237), A1 (07238), A2 (07239) and A3 (07240). The Trumpeter mouldings are sharp in this scale whilst a couple of details such as the ACAV's M60s' seem very bulky and lack the barrel. No driver position is modelled, and like *Italeri* the troop compartment lacks detailing. That said *Trumpeter* have included an engine which is a nice touch, and some careful cutting of certain panels will help reveal it. Instructions are as always clear, and the decals sharp and in register. If you're building the A3 ambulance version leave the commander's .50cal and mount off the finished model.

Chinese manufacturer *S-Model* provides three versions, the M132 flamethrower (No. SP072001), the Australian M113 with the T50 Gage turret (No. SP072002), and a special twin pack of the basic M113 (No. SP0720070). The hull is made up of three parts; lower, upper and engine bay, while the lower hull comprises of two quick build pieces, the main lower hull and the track and wheel assembly. Moulded in dark green plastic some details are sharp, others like the tracks are almost toy like.

It's fair to say that all three manufactures offerings have their merits and pit falls; the *S-Models* is great for a quick build and ease of construction, *Trumpeter's* inclusion of an engine and vinyl tracks following closely and *Italeri* offering interesting versions coming in close behind. In terms of presentation *S-Models* line drawing packaging isn't particularly inspiring, whilst *Trumpeter* has stayed with their photo top finishes used throughout their 1/72 range of afv's. *Italeri's* box finishes offer a hint of action with beautifully covers by the talented artist Giuseppe Rava who has rendered the M106 and M132 early 1980s MERDC camouflage beautifully as well as further images on the box sides and rear.

In 1/48 *Gaso.line* has produced two wonderful multi-part 1/48 examples of the M113. Both are rich in detail, with the Israeli Zelda (GAS50260) treated to interior detailing and appliqué armour whilst their other model is of a late Vietnam War ACAV (GAS50246K) complete with some excellent era relevant decals.

By far the largest selection of kits available is in 1/35. *Academy* offer three examples, all based on the main M113 chassis. The first is the M113A1 Vietnam version (13266). This provides the modeller with the choice of three finishes; the ACAV, the M132 flamethrower (extra

All above and left: Moulded in khaki plastic across two spures, Italeri's details are pretty standard for the scale.

Below: Gaso.line 50260 M113 Israeli Zelda.

Bottom: Gaso.line 50246K M113 late Vietnam War ACAV.

fuel tanks aren't supplied), and the Australian M50 Gage turret. Also included is a set of figures which gives the modeller the opportunity to create an interest vignette or small diorama straight from the box.

The M163 Vulcan (13507) is finished as the A1, however among the lavish spares an A2 or A3 can be built by adding the rear fuel tanks. The A3 Iraq Version (13211) includes the armoured commander's turret, spaced slat armour/exterior equipment stowage as well as the correct interior spall liners. A nice touch is the inclusion is a sprue of clear plastic bottles as well as decals for the field ambulance version.

All kits are in scale with great attention to detail and moulded in either beige or green plastic with the option to either use vinyl tracks or to make up lengths form individual pieces, however there are sink marks to deal with. Only the A1 Vietnam and A3 Iraq kits are supplied with engines. Instructions and decals are clear and sharp for all three and *Academy* has been generous in treating the modeller to some interesting parts for the spares box in all three kits.

AFV Club offer more eclectic variants of the M113, whilst they omit the engine from their kits the detailing is up to the usual high standards one expects from *AFV Club*. The IDF Nag'Mash (AF35311) is presented in grey plastic, well moulded and includes a small fret of Photo-etched parts that would make a stunning build for any IDF modeller.

Other kits include the M113A1 ACAV (AF35113), two versions of the YPR765 (AIFV) in Dutch service, the A1 (SFOR) (AF35119) and the basic PRI (Pantser-Rups-Infanterie) (AF35S14). Both are fitted with the 25mm KBA Cannon and come with early and late hull top options, as well as five different finishes.

AFV Club also offers the M548A1 (AF35003), and the M730 Chaparral (AF35002). The M548 is supplied with a load of shells, as well as markings for US, British, Australian and Bundeswehr use, also included is a length of chain for the rear-mounted chain hoist. Again construction is straight forward and the plastic is well moulded with the castings sharp. One final kit that really deserves a mention and whets the appetite is the M113 Gun-Truck Hybrid kit (AF35323). Perhaps the ultimate in Vietnam M113s, this kit screams out to be accompanied by GIs in its own action-filled diorama.

Instructions are always clear with some excellent referencing photography of key points for the modeller to be aware of and decals being well researched and beautifully printed. *AFV Club* moulds are stunning, with very little filling required, kits are supplied with flexible track. *AFV Club* also supply a series of detailing

kits including PE Mesh for the YPR765A1 (AG35017) and nicely moulded separate T130E1 track links and replacement sprocket and idler sets (AF35S22 & AF35306) as well as T130E1 and T150F track bands (AF35064-67). A wide range of decals are also produced enabling ROC Marine Corps low visibility types (TW60016).

Dragon have produced four interesting versions of the M113 family, including the M688 Lance Loader Transporter (DRA3607), M752 Lance Launcher (DR3576), M113 IDF (DRA3608) and a two-vehicle IDF combo featuring an M113 and the Chata'p Field Repair Vehicle (DRA3622), Sadly engines are omitted. All kits are moulded in grey plastic, featuring plastic tracks as straight runs with separate links for wrapping around the idler and sprocket wheels with vinyl track pads being supplied as extra elements. Kits also include PE for detailing tool clasps and strapping. Sadly instructions aren't the clearest so it pays to have a good look before committing yourself to action. That said decals are clear and in register and the finishes for the M688 include machines in use with the US and Bundeswehr.

German manufacture *Elite Models* offer both complete models and conversion kits of the M113 in Bundeswehr service. Kits are composed of resin, white metal, PE and vinyl parts and include the Beobachtungspanzer Artillerie M113GA2 (3503A), Mortar Carrier (35110) and the minelaying Scorpion based on the M548 (3514). These kits are complimented by a range of Bundeswehr-based conversions including the Command Post G3GE (3591a), and the M113 A2G ABRA Artillery Radar station (3552a). All kits and conversions come with Diehl's type 513B track and are based on *Tamiyas's* M113 and M577 kits.

Italeri have produced the ACAV (6506) and M163 VADS (6560) version of the M113. The ACAV features a host of spares, is well designed with a clear and concise instruction sheet with a wonderful decal sheet allowing the modeller to depict four in-theatre vehicles. Interior details are light but the enterprising modeller will soon be able to make or source PE and resin detailing to address this. The M163 is a far simpler and quicker build omitting interior details and finished for four separate versions, including early Vietnam use. Whilst sprues are packed with some great items and the mouldings are clear there is one or two awkwardly placed sink holes to be aware during the build.

Hobby Fan models are part of the AFV Club brand and produce limited-run resin and metal kits featuring plastic parts for the tracks and details such as lights as well as AFV Club decals. Kits include the British Tracked Rapier (HF086), M667 Lance Guided Missile Carrier (HF034) and the M113 Lynx Command Vehicle (HF022). Each model is well researched and the resin finish is of the highest quality. Hobby Fan also produces two conversion sets for M113; the TOW/ CM25 (HF031) and the M163 Vulcan (HF036). Both kits are exceptionally well appointed, though expect to some surgery, especially with the M163 conversion.

Tamiya have no less than four kits based on their original 1974 M113 (3540), all are developments of this venerable kit which features a full, if somewhat basic, interior. The kits are presented in boxes with artwork by Yoshiyuki Takani and Masami Onishi. The ACAV (35135) continues the use of the interior fittings along with a sheet of gauze for the all-important anti-RPG fence and decals for cola cans and cigarette packets. The A2 (35265) and M577 Command Post (35071) versions are quick build types with no interior fittings for, however the extra stowage items included in the A2 make up for this. As always the instructions and decals are clear and well researched but sadly some of the moulding finishes are a little rough, with moulds showing their age. Whilst easily rectified, the numerous sink holes are a little annoying, but once addressed present a nice little model. Tracks are of the vinyl type, and not as sharp as contemporary offerings. Figures are included with all kits so you can easily build a diorama or vignette straight out of the box.

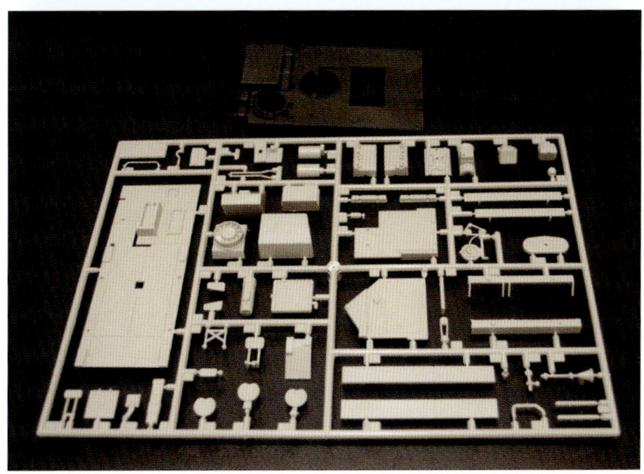

Conversion and Detailing Kits

It's the vast array of aftermarket parts which the M113 enjoys, with numerous PE packages, resin and the growing range of 3D conversions there is something for everyone. Here follows a list of suppliers who currently make these items that help bring your model alive. Due to the almost endless list of kits available and to save on confusion I have identified those which really will whet the appetite and prompt the modeller into looking at the myriad of opportunities available. Unless otherwise stated all scales are 1/35.

Accurate Armour (AA) has produced several resin and PE kits for Tamiya and Academy's M113 models. As well as series of ACAV shields (C003/4) *AA* have also produced conversion sets to allow modeller the opportunity to model M113's in Australian LRV (C015), Israeli (C016) and Danish (C080) service. Also available is a set of semi-flexible (T05) T130E1 track. As always, items are finely moulded and well researched.

Airwaves are renowned for their competitively priced and easy to use PE sets aimed at the more cautious modeller. For the M113 they offer two sets of well researched PE for Academy's M113 to either Israeli standard (AC35032), with the side cages for extra armour. Set AC35015 offers antenna protectors and internal strapping for the standard M113.

Black Dog have gone to town with their predominantly IDF based 1/72 resin and PE conversion kits including an experimental turreted version (T72035). A single conversion kit (T72015) is available for the A3 fitted with the commanders ACAV armoured turret and crews personal kit. The 1/35 conversion kits include the M163 (T35185), the Zelda 2 (T35094) for the *Academy* kit, and the six wheeled Australian Armoured Logistics Vehicle (ALV) (T35206) for *Tamiya* kits. The kits are well researched and the castings sharp, offering the modeller some great opportunities to create a well stocked motor pool of variants.

Callsign models are an Australian company producing some resin, brass and PE extras for Vietnam era M113's including interior sandbag floor (CS35023) and mine damaged road wheels (35019). Three conversion sets, all for *Tamiya's* M113 track the development of the Australian M113 in Vietnam; CS35022 is based on the first M113s in service, CS35070 features the early Gage T-50 turret models and CS35069 the late 1970 version. In the case of the T-50 models the details of these turrets are breathtaking, and the models would sit well with contemporary Centurions and infantry in a themed diorama. Callsign also produces three gun shields for the commander's position (CS35024,31,32) as simple update kits.

It has to be said that once again *Eduard's* team led by Vladimir Sulc, have gone all out producing over 25 PE sets for the M113 family. Both interior and exterior details have been made, as well as wheel masks for *AFV Club, Academy, Italeri, Revell* and *Tamiya* M113s. Given the sharpness of today's models Eduard's offerings are increasingly about bringing vintage kits slap band up to date, giving the modeller both challenges and satisfaction of upgrading their M113. *Eduard* remain the byword for excellence in PE; well designed, well researched and well made kit instruction are a joy to use and really help make the perfect M113.

Firestorm Models produce two simple resin updates for the M113 in Australian service, the first is the important Vietnam era belly armour update (FS35066), and the Low Rounded Gun shield (FS35067). Sharply cast in resin, the belly armour in particular is a welcome update to Vietnam era M113's.

Korean after-market masters *Legend* are prolific producers of some of the finest aftermarket kits on offer today. These multimedia kits are awash with detail, often accompanied by excellent PE with delicate decals that turn a kit into a work of art. The M113 family have received the full treatment from Canadian A3's (LF1318) and ADATS (LF1286) to the IDF fitters vehicle with HIAB crane (LF1387) Legend have produced no less than fifteen kits for the M113. These kits are for the experienced modeller, requiring patience and skill, with sometimes ambiguous instruction, but don't let that stop you trying to create your own masterpiece.

Russian white metal track manufacture *Master Club* produce two different type of T130E1 track for the M113; MTL35113 with pristine track pads and MTL35114 with worn out pads. Kits are nicely designed with the tracks and vinyl pads being two separate parts with tracks held together with tapered plastic pins. Assembly requires a steady hand, but the effects are worth it.

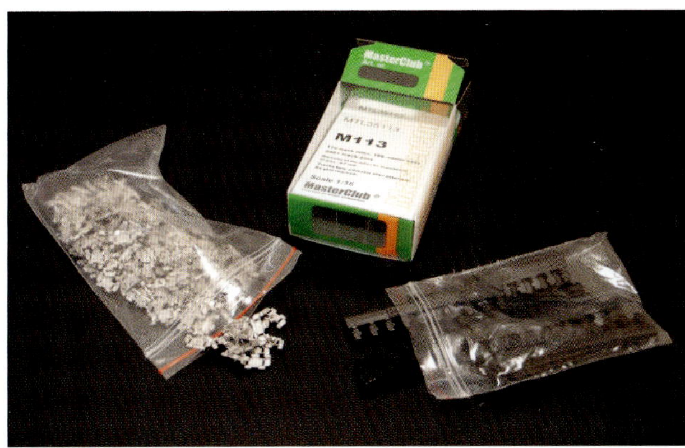

MMK produce two resin and PE details and conversion kits for the M113 family; the Australian Gage T-50 turret (F3048) and the rarely seen IDF SAMSON RCWS 30 remote turret (F3060) and both fit *Academy*, *Italeri*, and *Tamiya* M113s. Parts are clearly cast and etched and the instructions are wonderfully clear, with excellent photography throughout to guide the builder thought these complex builds.

MR Modellbau produce parts and conversions for the M113, as well as standalone 1/87 models. Kits including the 120mm M1064A3 mortar in Bundeswehr service (35074) conversion set for *Tamiya*'s M106 and updates for M113's in Swiss (35067) and Canadian service (35242). 1/87 models include a Danish PNMK with 25mm Oerlikon gun (87134) and the Israeli mobile workshop (87062) as well as much needed interior fittings. Mouldings are sharp for all scales and the conversion kits are straightforward enough.

Panzer Art have produced several resin kits for the M113; the sandbag roof protection kit (RE35-595) and road wheels (RE35-494) for US M113's and two sandbag protection kits for IDF vehicles (RE35-158 and 232). As with all *Panzer Art* resin the items are well researched, and cleanly moulded, especially the sandbag protection kits.

Perfect Scale Modellbau produce full resin conversion and detailing kits including the six-wheeled M113 G3 (35056). Using *Academy*'s M113 kit as the donor for all its conversions including the M901 ITV (35065) and the M981 FISTV (35066), modellers can also use *Italeri*'s M113 as the base for the conversions. Kits are well researched and detailing is sharp. *Perfect Scale Modellbau* also produces a wonderful multimedia M113 Lynx complete with UN decals and the correct Diehl tracks.

Terre Models have produced a complete interior set for Tamiya's M577 Command Post (TM009). It features an engine, driver's compartment and fully appointed command post complete with radios, map drawers, seating and the all-important field phone. As the interiors of the command post were pretty generic, this kit will suit the M577 in service with a range of countries. The mouldings are exceptionally sharp and the instructions are concise and clear.

Voyager have produced five PE sets for *AFV Club* and *Tamiya* M113s which cover early and A1 versions of the APC, including the ACAV (PE35801 and 913), early IDF Nagmash M113s (PE35805) and the later A2 (PE35382). All kits are well researched with clear and straight forward instructions, though occasional translations errors means the modeller may have to use the visual guides as prompts. *Voyager* deliver some great PE and for those not quite confident to go the whole hog, they supply a small fret of engine cover grills (FE35035) to help the modeller get used to working with metal.

Decals

All decals in this section have been specifically designed for use with the M113 family, covering the type throughout the 20th and 21st centuries. Unless noted otherwise all decals are in 1/35.

Archer Transfers offers the modeller generic M113 (AR35333/356) and M106 (AR35333) based English language stencils for both interior and exterior use as well as a series of Arabic language decals (AR35063B/63W) for use with vehicles used during the Lebanese conflicts in particular.

Black Lion Decals produce two sets of decals for the YPR-765; 35024/25. The first features SFOR, domestic and ISAF marking for the turreted version whilst the second features markings for the *Koninklijke Marechausse* or Royal Military Police and ambulance versions. Nicely finished, *Black Lion Decals* have got the tone of the whites and yellows absolutely spot on.

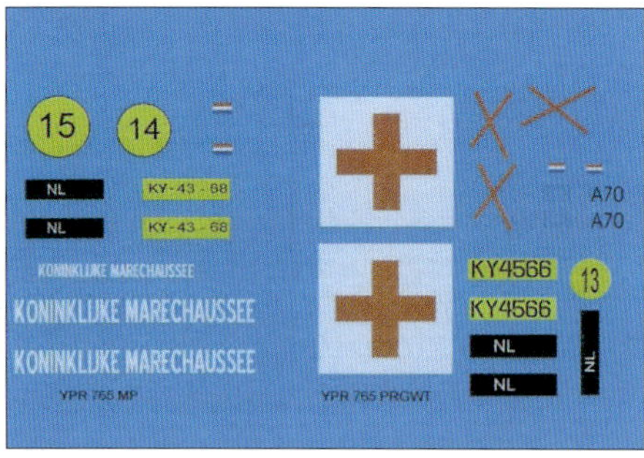

Bison Decals have produced two sets of decals for IDF M113s; the first covers the period from the Yom Kippur War to the 1978 Lebanon War (35174), the second (35189),   cover the 1982 Lebanese conflict. Both include detailed views of vehicles used, including painting guides. The yellows are strong with blacks rendered at 90% grey.

Echelon have focused their output on the Vietnam conflict with decals sheets often shared among varying types of vehicles used by specific units, especially cavalry units. For more contemporary marking the 20th Engineer Battalion are treated to their own set (D356089) whilst set D356056 provides Red Cross marking for A3 field ambulances. A set

is also made for IDF MEDEVAC M113s featuring the IDF's Red Star of David emblem (D356138). One final innovation for the modeller of modern M113s is the pink periscope surface inserts which simulate the anti-laser coating applied to modern periscopes.

FC Modeltips produce decals for the M113 in Spanish military service as well as a range of 3D printed detailing parts, a trend that is growing as the technology becomes more refined. The decals are for the recently formed branch of the Spanish Armed Forces, the *Unidad Militar de Emergencias* (UME) (C35219) or Military Emergencies who are responsible for providing disaster relief primarily in Spain as well as examples for the Infantry (35221) which has markings for no less then 15 vehicles and a set for the cavalry (35226) with markings for 14 individual vehicles.

The 3D parts, which are made to order, come as four separate sets covering the ACAV, M113, A1 and A2 versions. One set that will be of interest to modellers is set 35451 featuring the rear bilge vent pipe and inlet and exhaust pipes for the interior heater.

Greek decal makers *LM Decals* produce decals for M113's and M106's in Hellenic service in both 1/72 and 1/35 scales as well as generic decals in 1/87. These include national symbols as well as KFOR and EOD markings. Sharp and well designed these decals would suit a Balkans diorama beautifully.

MECModels produce decals in 1/72 and 1/35 for the M113 family focusing their efforts on the often amazing graffiti, giving the modeller beautifully rendered and produced decals. Be aware some of the terminology and imagery is of its time and modeller discretion is advised.

Olds Models have produced decals in 1/72 and 1/35 for the M113 in New Zealand army service (OMD1175). Included are 'UN' markings, names and numerals which are clearly printed.

Star Decals have a prolific range of markings for the M113 in a range of roles, including the Gun-Truck Hybrid (35-C1176-78), the M577 and M132 (35-932) and ACAV's in US Airborne service (35-931). Star has also produce decals for Lebanese (35-959) and Israeli M113s (35-C 1157). The decals are well researched and finely printed with yellows consistently sharp and the blacks never more than 80% grey. The range is well worth investigating as it covers differing types, opening up a host of diorama detailing options.

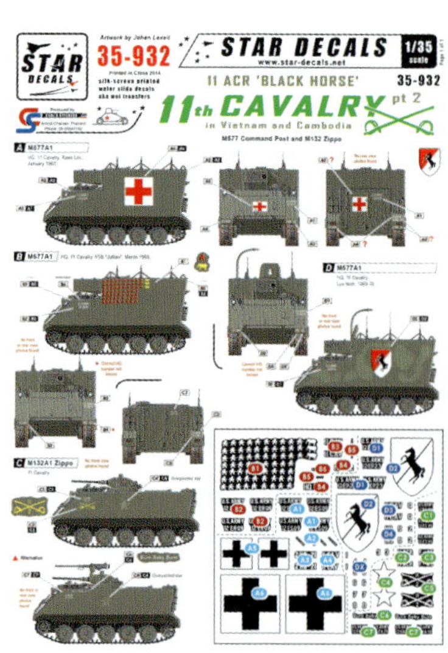